UNDERSTANDING THE EDUCATION
— AND THROUGH IT THE CULTURE —
IN EDUCATION ABROAD

D0219383

Understanding the Education

—and through it the culture—

in Education Abroad

by

Linda A. Chisholm and Howard A. Berry

with a foreword by

Margaret D. Pusch

The International Partnership for Service-Learning
New York, New York

The International Partnership for Service-Learning
815 Second Avenue, Suite 315
New York, NY 10017 USA

LCCN 2002115732
ISBN 0-9701984-3-4

Book design and cover art by Kate Chisholm

Printed on acid-free paper

First Edition

To the memory and work of

HOWARD A. BERRY

1932 – 2002

Pioneer in international education

and service-learning

Table of Contents

Foreword

Study abroad is not a process of gathering credit in another country but of being part of another academic and social culture while continuing the work of being a student. When you think of all the adaptations students must make, it is no wonder they return home changed in their ways of thinking and in their perceptions of the world around them. The outward signs (language facility, new hairstyle) of the "foreign" influence is little more than a veneer covering the shifts in attitude, world view, and personal insight that often accompany immersion in another culture. Through the experience abroad, students have not only gained that important credit but learned to steer their way through a place significantly unlike "home."

It is difficult to understand a new culture by attempting, simultaneously, to comprehend all its practices, customs, institutions, and other visible cultural constructions, let alone the values and beliefs that lie beneath their surfaces. It is extremely difficult to swallow a culture whole and try to make sense out of all the seemingly disparate, and sometimes contradictory, parts of it. The approach advocated in this book narrows the search.

Since institutions reflect the culture in which they are located, studying one in depth provides a path through which the secrets of a culture can be explored. The institution selected for the process explained here is higher education, the one with which arriving students will have an inevitable and close encounter. The rewards of pursuing the study recommended here are twofold, as both the institutional and cultural systems the student is living and studying in become less mysterious and forbidding. As Linda Chisholm states, "Education both reflects and shapes a society," so while education is a subset of the society, it is also a repository of its cultural knowledge. Within walls that may not be covered with ivy, stories are told, through courses in the sciences, liberal arts, and various professional schools, that explain what is important in the culture, and heroes are honored as an example of how best to contribute to the society. The manner in which the institution and even schedules are organized, how the faculty relates to students and colleagues, what holidays are celebrated, the architecture, extracurricular activities, and "normal" student behavior are all grist for the culture-discovery mill. It is equally interesting to uncover what the local students intend to do after they graduate, how they selected a course of study, and how they determined what their life work might be. There is a wealth of information about the culture just waiting to be plumbed from exploring this institution alone, but the research will inevitably lead into the larger culture.

This book is a "syllabus" for learning from the adventure of entering a strange country, culture, and school and for guiding the study abroad student toward a more rewarding and richer experience. It provides a framework in which to deposit the bits of information gleaned from day-to-day life as a student and connecting them with the content of academic study.

The field has long awaited materials that provide a systematic way of investigating a readily available resource for culture learning. The qualifications and experience of Linda Chisholm and the late Howard Berry made them uniquely positioned to create these materials. They have explored academic systems as well as local service organizations throughout the world while developing partnerships between institutions in higher education, community organizations, and The International Partnership for Service-Learning. Their approach is one of building relationships, getting to know the people who lead universities and faculty who are in the classroom as a way of finding out how the institutions work and how well students are encouraged to learn and reflect on their experience. They have always been educators who taught as if students were in the room, finding ways of engaging students in their own learning rather than teaching at them.

Telling the student to use his or her own university in the destination country as an entry point into the culture may be good advice, but is hardly sufficient for guiding them through that process. Most students want clear "directions" for being in a new culture, something that is impossible to furnish. This book provides directions for learning the culture, a skill that will be useful over and over again. Most study abroad advisors would prefer to do more than manage recruitment, logistics, and orientation. This book provides a means for focusing on being international educators in a way that fits the students' need to know more about where they are going. It is a highly portable, admittedly unusual, and very valuable guide.

Margaret (Peggy) Pusch
Portland, Oregon
October 20, 2002

Acknowledgments

The authorship of this little book needs explaining. Howard Berry is co-author and yet he is not. He wrote and submitted the proposal to NAFSA: Association of International Educators, through which the project was funded and launched. He wrote much of the letter to advisors. He had ideas about many of the chapters and he wrote parts of several. He and I presented the material contained in this book at a Region X conference of NAFSA in the fall of 2001 in Poughkeepsie, New York.

It is impossible to identify who first conceived the idea for the project. Howard Berry and I worked side by side for over twenty years, first imagining, then developing The International Partnership for Service-Learning. In the very beginning, we were co-chairs of a task force; then, in The Partnership's infancy, we were its co-directors. By the early 1990's, as The Partnership reached its maturity, the board of trustees (with my full support) named Howard the first president and me the vice president. Our close professional collaboration of daily interaction meant that we usually could not remember who originated an idea, whether it was for the conceptual basis on which The International Partnership has been built; for its fourteen international programs uniting academic study and volunteer service; or for the development of the organization. Often, of course, it came from neither of us, but rather from one of our colleagues on the board of trustees, our program directors, or the now thousands of Partnership students.

Howard Berry died suddenly and unexpectedly on January 20, 2002. We were planning to spend the following day, the Martin Luther King, Jr., holiday, working on this project.

And so I write what many other authors have said in the acknowledgments of their books, but which I have a special reason to write and emphasize: If this project has merit, it is shared by Howard and me; if it has faults, they are entirely my own.

Howard would want to join me in expressing appreciation to the many professionals and students who have contributed to the project:

The U.S. Department of State and NAFSA: Association of International Educators for support of the project. NAFSA administers the program of COOP grants, funded in part by the Bureau of Educational and Cultural Affairs of the U.S. Department of State, under the authority of the Fulbright-Hays Act of 1961 (as amended).

Especially appreciated are the work of Emily Mohajeri Norris, Christine Jarchow, Elizabeth Smiltneek, and Elizabeth Schultz of the Student/Community Linkage Programs of NAFSA.

Margaret D. Pusch, former president of NAFSA and vice chair of the board of trustees of The International Partnership for Service-Learning, for writing the forword to the book.

Partnership program directors, especially Marie Cerna, Charles University, Czech Republic; Maria del Carmen Molestina and Diego Quiroga, Universidad San Francisco de Quito, Ecuador; Chantal Thery, Université Montpellier II, France; Veta Lewis,

University of Technology, Jamaica; Erlinda Rosales, Trinity College of Quezon City, Philippines; Valerian Three Irons, South Dakota State University, United States.

Kate Chisholm for editing, layout, and cover design; and Kate Egan Norris for copyediting.

Introduction for Advisors

Dear Study Abroad and Foreign Student Advisors,

This book has two purposes. The first, as the name suggests, is to help students learn about and reflect upon the new culture they will be entering when they go abroad to study. The means for this increased understanding is the study of a topic that will be close at hand — higher education. The second purpose of the book is directed to you as a professional educator, giving you a resource and a practical plan for enhancing your current role and effectiveness.

Students' learning through education abroad

A majority of students engaging in education abroad, whether by leaving the United States or coming to the U.S. from another country, take college/university classes at an in-country institution where they are taught by in-country faculty. This design is not only common but favored and encouraged. It is emphasized in program materials as an advantage and strength because it allows the students to experience the host culture directly rather than having it interpreted through a faculty member from the student's home country.

And yet, oddly, there generally is little or no preparation given to the students about the cultural rationale behind the system of education they will enter. They go abroad and participate in the studies with no real knowledge of the background of the educational system of their host country. Even after many

1

months abroad they have only a glimmer of understanding of why it is designed as it is, what historical, social, political, and religious forces may have shaped it, and what purposes it is meant to serve. They do not realize that behind different curricula and methods of teaching are a series of assumptions about desired outcomes. They understand little about the social and economic background of their fellow students or the place the particular institution where they are studying fits into the national picture of higher education in their host country. As a result, students often participate in the classes and studies at face value, without realizing the larger and richer implications for their understanding of the host culture.

They return home, and when asked about their experience abroad, they speak glowingly of how much the overall experience meant to them. But they are often silent about their academic experience or indicate only that it was "OK." It is possible that the other experiences of living abroad are the stimulating ones for them, that they simply take the university setting as a given, something not unlike home, to be endured for the sake of the more exciting things.

A closer probing, however, also reveals that, either voluntarily or when asked, they commonly cite problems in this area. These include comments such as "The faculty didn't teach the way I am used to." " I couldn't figure out what my teacher expected of me." " My teachers were better (or worse) than my teachers at home." " They required us to buy books to which they never subsequently referred." " I was criticized for the way I dressed for class." " My teachers didn't understand that sharing of and collaboration on schoolwork among students is the expected procedure in my home country." (This last statement is most often heard from students coming to the U.S.)

Faculty members have their counterpart responses. While they report enjoying teaching students from other nations, they also report problems in getting students to adhere to the requirements, standards, and behavior they expect. They report that these problems become obstacles to a successful academic experience and interaction, as well as causing the students to miss an important element of cultural learning and thereby failing to arrive at a more sophisticated understanding of the host society.

Educational systems are one of the most important institutions of a society, reflecting strongly, in microcosm, the cultural norms and values of the larger society. Students who engage in study abroad are missing a golden opportunity to encounter and understand their host culture if they do not see the educational experience as equal to the home stays, travel, field trips, internships, service, and any other aspects of the program.

This book is based on these simple, yet profound, premises:

- Education both reflects and shapes a culture.
- Studying, analyzing, and understanding the system of education is an excellent way to understand the culture.
- The study (like any study worth the name) must be deliberate and sustained, so that conclusions are based not on a few isolated incidents but on a systematic and thorough examination of the topic.
- Learning how to see the culture, its values and norms, its beliefs and expectations through the examination of one of its social systems—education—is a skill transferable to other institutions of the society such as the economy, the health-care system, family patterns, or social structures. It is a skill transferable to other

cultures as well, whether these are the macro-cultures of a religion, region or nation or the micro-culture culture of a particular business or extended family.

- Possessing this skill makes one more understanding of others' behavior and values, more capable of compassion, and more able to negotiate settlements satisfactory to all parties. In short, this skill is a characteristic of an educated and civilized person and leader.

Your professional role in education abroad

As important as the first theme of this book is, the second — your professional role — is even more important. Howard Berry and I presented this material at the NAFSA: Association of International Educators' Region X Conference in November, 2001, in Poughkeepsie, New York. It was voted the regional highlight and thus was selected for presentation at the national conference of NAFSA held in May, 2002, in San Antonio, Texas. At both meetings I began by asking the audience a few questions. "How many of you are study abroad advisors?" Most were. "How many of you are foreign-student advisors?" Almost all of the remaining participants held up their hands. Now an either/or question: "How many of you believe that you are perceived on your campus as an educator or teacher and how many believe you are perceived as an administrator or paper-processor? A twitter of nervous laughter was followed by an overwhelming vote for the latter.

Sadly, shockingly, you seem to agree that your faculty colleagues on campus do not understand that your role is no less important than theirs, and that, in fact, you should be full partners in directing the education of the students. After all, you are responsible for one-eighth or even one-fourth of their undergraduate education!

The underlying assumption of colleges and universities is that the study of any subject is greatly enhanced by the help of a teacher. We provide libraries, laboratories, the Internet and performance studios. But most of all we provide teachers. We know that students are capable of reading widely and deeply on their own, but it is the teachers who give structure, meaning, and order to the overwhelming array of information. It is the teachers who ask the probing questions leading to more sophisticated analysis. It is the teachers who suggest guidelines for judging the worth of theories, studies, and reports.

If studying in a different country is to be the rich educational experience we claim it can be, all of us in study abroad advising should be active players. We must claim our role as educators and teachers. This book is meant to be a resource for you to do just that.

As stated above, it is based on a simple yet profound premise: that the educational system of a nation reflects and shapes a culture. When students understand this concept and make an intentional study of the higher education system in which they find themselves, their understanding of the society is deepened and enriched. This guide is a means for them to organize and round out the information and experience that will come to them in bits and pieces throughout their study abroad.

Ideally, there would be a teacher in their institution abroad who would guide their analysis of education and therefore of the culture. But that is unlikely to be the case. If they are enrolled in a university and this kind of study is not part of the regular courses offered, then you cannot expect the students to find help abroad for this study.

What we want to propose to you is that you consider making this study a requirement for all of your students who go abroad to study or come from another country to study here. You can and should be the teacher, facilitator, mentor, and guide. The use of e-mail will allow you to monitor your students' progress as they first submit reports of critical incidents, then the summary of interviews and research, and finally a substantial term paper for your evaluation. In it they would be required to describe all the topics outlined in this guide, show how the institution at which they are studying is representative or not representative of the educational system of the country, and then demonstrate how the educational system they are encountering both reflects and shapes the culture. For a good paper, with all the academic requirements of solid research, the student should be awarded three credits as part of the student's degree program. The students will, after all, have been engaged in the "field study" for this assignment almost every waking moment during their semester or year abroad!

You should be given faculty status—and faculty compensation—for guiding their study. You will be the teacher and the evaluator. You are the expert on study abroad and are familiar, at least in general, with educational systems of other nations. In terms of the institution's organizational structure, you should be "located" for this responsibility in a department, which could be history, sociology, education or international/intercultural studies.

The student might also use the paper as the basis for a senior or honors paper, with a second study—that of the student's home institution and system—forming a comparative study.

I urge you to claim your territory! You are an educator, responsible for ensuring that students who go abroad make the most of their experience. You must exercise your role as a teacher and you deserve to be recognized as one by your institution.

Linda A. Chisholm and Howard A. Berry

Introduction for Students

Dear Student,

So you are going to study abroad! You have surfed the web, consulted with your study abroad advisor, chosen a country and a foreign university, talked to your parents, filled out the forms, and sent in your application. You have received a letter of acceptance and your college or university has approved your plan. Congratulations!

Now you are packing your bags, buying your plane ticket, obtaining your passport, and saying good-bye to friends and family. What an exciting time you expect to have, meeting new people, seeing new sights, speaking a language not your own or learning a variation of your native language! You will be on a new campus, studying new subjects, with new teachers and new friends. In not many months, you will have learned to get around and get along in your new country, and you will think of yourself correctly as a citizen of the world.

One important dimension of your study abroad will be your encounter with a new system of higher education. It may, at first glance, appear to be similar to home. There will be campus buildings, libraries, classrooms, laboratories, recital halls, a computer center, and sports fields. You will begin to meet teachers, administrators, support staff, and your fellow students.

But the reality is that you will be in a system of higher education that is quite different from the one to which you are accustomed.

9

Students returning from a semester or year of studying abroad tell us that if they had understood from the beginning that there would be differences, they would have learned more and gotten along better. Sadly, a few students never understand the differences or how to deal with them, and they find their study abroad fraught with difficulties to the point that they do not enjoy the experience. Sometimes, frankly, the host country teachers and students wish they had stayed home.

It was returning students who first suggested to us at The International Partnership for Service-Learning that we develop a guide to help students analyze the differences between higher education in their home college or university and that in their host country and institution. This book is the result. It is meant to help chart your way through the rocks and shoals, not giving you answers, but providing a series of topics with examples to guide your observations and conclusions about your education abroad. We hope it will make the journey smoother for you, and help you get the most out of the marvelous experience you are about to have.

Take a few moments to recall how you felt when you first arrived from high school at your home college or university. There were new words whose meaning you had to learn— words such as "matriculation," "majors," "minors," " courses," and "prerequisites." You may have found that the word "discipline" means something quite different from what it meant in lower school!

You had to learn how to read the catalog—what courses you were allowed to take as a first-year student and which ones had to wait until you had acquired the necessary background in a subject. You probably encountered new words and new concepts to describe the various subjects that are taught as well as the names and subject matter of disciplines and of subsets within the disciplines.

As you began classes, you may also have found that your relationship to your teachers was quite different from those with your secondary school teachers. The library was undoubtedly larger than you had previously encountered and you had to learn your way around it. The pattern of classes, the requirements for writing papers, the form of examinations, and the criteria for grading were new as well. You may have had to master the forms for properly acknowledging the ideas of other authors and learn when you are required to make such citations.

In addition to these academic issues you had other needs, and you set about finding where you could turn for advice and help. You located the housing department and the financial aid office. You investigated extracurricular activities such as sports teams, service clubs, music and drama groups, and you got involved. You were probably assigned an academic advisor who helped you select the course of study you would follow.

Now you will be repeating the process of discovery and learning, except that you will be doing this in a new country, culture, and institution of higher education.

You succeeded in learning these things when you first entered higher education. Why, you ask, do you need to investigate the system of higher education in your new environment?

Quite simply, you need to make a conscious and deliberate effort to understand the system of higher education in your new country because, although you are going from a college or university in your home country to a college or university in another country, you will find there are many, many differences. To get the most out of your education abroad, to adjust quickly, and to succeed in your academic work, you need to realize that you are operating in a system as different from your institution at home as your high school was from your home college or university. When you do not expect differences, you can easily fall into believing that the same assumptions and practices you have come to expect at home are in operation abroad. You tend to look for similarities—and you will find them. But the differences in assumptions, in systems, and in relationships can be crucial.

If you have traveled abroad, you know that people your age may wear the same style and even brands of clothing. They may eat the same foods and listen to the same music. But you know that they are not the same. Their life values, their ambitions, their families, their religion, and their politics may be vastly different.

This little book is meant to help you analyze the differences in education between that of your home country and what you experience abroad. It is meant to help you suspend judgment until you discover—uncover!—both the expectations and the behavior of those you meet in your education abroad.

But the book is meant to do more than smooth your way. It is meant to help you understand your host culture more deeply by helping you understand its system of higher education. Throughout your reflection on education, there is one underlying premise that should be constantly on your mind. You will find it repeated throughout this book.

Education both reflects and shapes a society.

As you come to understand education in your new country, keep asking how the values and systems you are encountering reflect the characteristics you are discovering about the society in which you are living. Higher education is a subset of a society and the institution you attend is but one example of that subset, sharing characteristics with other institutions of higher education, but probably in some ways remaining distinctive. You will need to be careful and sophisticated about how you relate the education you experience abroad to the values, customs, beliefs, and expectations of the larger society. Careful observation and thorough analysis will help you to understand your host culture more completely.

And, we assume that higher education leaves its mark. How will the educational system form those who pass through it? What belief and qualities are your classmates acquiring that will in turn shape their society as they become its leaders in the future?

Finally, and not least important, how will your study abroad inform and change you? How might you and your educational experience abroad influence your home society?

Make the most of the education as you embark on your journey of education abroad. Happy sailing!

Linda A. Chisholm

Chapter 1

Gathering and Assessing Information

To learn about and understand higher education in your host culture and to see how it reflects and shapes the culture you will have three valuable sources of information: What you see, what you hear, and what you read.

What you see

From the moment you arrive on campus in your host country, you will be observing and comparing. In the beginning it will be enough to be aware of and take note of differences you observe between what you have experienced previously in higher education and what you are experiencing in your host institution abroad. Later you will want to consider these comparisons as a means of understanding your host—and home—education and the culture that they reflect.

> **Example**: Are the facilities and equipment equal or superior to those on your home campus? A U.S. student from a very fine Quaker-based college was awestruck upon seeing the gorgeous buildings at a university in Mexico and then critical when she realized that the library holdings of her small college outnumbered those of the Mexican university. Later, as she knew more about the history of Mexico and reflected on the comparative values of the two cultures, she understood that simplicity of life is a Quaker virtue, while impres-

sive public architecture has been an important value in Aztec, Spanish, and Mexican culture for at least ten centuries.

What you hear

Whether in the dining hall, the local pub, or the dormitories, with the teacher after class, the personnel of your overseas program, or on radio or television, you will be hearing about higher education. Organize your questions and ask for interviews with people at your host university and elsewhere. If you tell them you are engaged in a formal study of higher education in their country, they will take your effort seriously and come prepared to answer your questions or direct you to the answers.

As you progress in your study you may find that some of your sources of information are very reliable and others less so. This is true of all sources of information but especially of conversations and interviews. Your informant may or may not be knowledgeable and accurate. As your study of higher education develops, you will need to check the accuracy of what you are hearing.

Example: Your fellow students in the dormitories or whom you meet in the dining hall may be able to tell you a great deal, and accurately, about the preparation of students for university. But they may know very little about the percentage of their age cohort who enter higher education or the numbers of those who graduate. The accuracy of their answers may, in fact, say something about class differences in the host society. All of us, including students, are often quite unaware of people in our own country whose lives have not

16

intersected with our own. We tend to move in our own social, economic, and educational circles. University students are likely to overestimate the percent of young people in their nation who engage in higher education on the inaccurate basis that most of their own friends and schoolmates did in fact go on to university.

What you read

Your sources should include the college catalog and any other printed or web-posted material—the college newspaper, books, and newspapers—published by your institution and others. Most countries have journals about education. Newspapers often have sections set aside for education reporting. Ask about major reports that may have been released recently.

Example: In the U.S., the *Chronicle of Higher Education,* which appears weekly, will be in the college library and in the offices of a number of administrators and faculty members. The *Dearing Report* in England, which was released in 1999, is having a significant impact on the structure and goals of higher education in Great Britain.

Organizing your study

As you begin to gather information to build your understanding of the education in your education abroad, you should recognize that the process will not be a linear one. (Learning almost never is, despite our training as heirs of Descartes and the Enlightenment!) Through your observations, your conversations, and your reading related to higher education in your host culture, you will be gathering a tidbit on one topic here and a morsel on another topic there. Information will be coming to you randomly at first.

Think of approaching your study of higher education as you would approach a giant jigsaw puzzle. Your job is to bring order—to make a picture—of many small pieces. Just as you would in working a puzzle, you begin by placing a few pieces on the edge. This small piece is about students, that one about faculty. As you find more and more pieces and put them in categories, you will find the picture you are building becoming clear.

If you have been diligent in gathering and recording information, you will find that about two-thirds of the way through your semester or year abroad, you need to assess the information you have gathered and begin a systematic search to fill in the remaining holes. You may have completed the corner of the picture having to do with students, but need to intentionally read about the history of higher education.

When doing a jigsaw puzzle, you can't complete the picture if you're missing some of the pieces. For this picture-making, puzzle-solving process, you must arrange the pieces you gather along the way so that you don't lose any of them. Likewise with your research, to make the most of the information in order later to organize and process it, you must develop a system of making notes. The chapters to follow are organized by topic. You should keep a loose-leaf notebook following the order of the chapters so that all the notes you make on a given topic can be grouped together.

> **Example**: Even before you leave home, or while you're on the airplane, you may discover information in the college/university catalog about such varying topics as the purposes of higher education as seen in your host culture, the content of the curriculum, the requirements for graduation, the qualifications and

training of the faculty, and the ways the subjects and disciplines are taught.

Careful reading will raise questions for you, questions you may wish later to pursue.

Example: Note how many of the faculty are men and how many are women. Ask yourself if this is revealing of the definition of gender roles in the society that you are entering. But beware! This information may or may not paint a true and complete picture of the situation in the wider culture you are entering. There are subtleties. The university abroad may have a small percentage of women because the average age of the faculty is high. Opportunities for women scholars may have changed in recent decades. As the current senior (male) faculty members retire, they may be being replaced by young women, so that the relation of men to women in the faculty may change dramatically in the next few years. Suspend judgment until you have investigated further and can be confident of your conclusions.

Those of you who have studied anthropology or any subject requiring field study know that as you gather information and keep notes, you must make sure that you also record the source of each item and the date the observation occurred. If it is written information, note the date of publication. As you study higher education you will also be developing your critical and analytical skills. In the beginning, especially if you are speaking a language not native to you, you may simply be misunderstanding what you are hearing or reading. But even if you are speaking and hearing a language in which you are fluent, you may be unfamiliar with the special terminology of education.

Example: In Britain or a British-derived system, the word "course" refers to a three-year program of study leading to the degree. In the United States and in U.S.-based education, "course" refers to a much smaller unit of study, usually about one-fortieth of the program for the Bachelor's Degree.

Armed with a notebook and this guide, you are ready to begin your investigation of education abroad and, through it, the culture.

Chapter 2

First Things First

In working a jigsaw puzzle, you begin by identifying the pieces that will make up corners and straight edges. You build a frame into which you will fit other pieces. If it is a complex puzzle, the frame may not tell you much about what the final picture will portray.

In working your puzzle of higher education, your corners and straight edges will be the questions for which you should be able to find answers in the first days of your program. They not only begin to build your frame but will smooth your transition, helping you succeed in both your academic work and in your relationships with people at your host university or college abroad.

A short program has probably been arranged to introduce you to the educational experience you are entering. Your home institution may have such a program and then you will have a second one when you arrive in the country. These programs are very useful, but you will probably not be told everything you need to know without your asking. You must be active in the process. Use the occasion(s) to ask your questions.

Remember the words at the end of the previous chapter, advising you to be sure you know the meaning of the words used.

Example: In the U.S., we call these introductory programs "orientation." In Britain and many other places, they are called "induction programmes." The U.S. uses the word "induction" to refer to entry into the military forces. If you are entering a British or British-derived system of higher education, rest assured that you are not being pressed into service in the Royal Army!

Classes and course work

You will want to know the classes you will take. In some programs these will be determined in advance. They may be a set of integrated studies (usually related to the culture) or there may be options from a limited list. This will be probably be the case if you are studying at a university where the primary language is not yours but which offers some courses in your language. If you are enrolling in an institution where you will be taking the same classes as the local students you may have a wide range of options, just as you would at your home college or university.

If you are to be studying in a language not your own, you should be aware that you may run into difficulties. Students (and their home teachers) often overestimate their ability to manage classes and assignments in a foreign language. Many university level courses are difficult enough to follow even in one's native language. Understanding the regional dialect of professors and local students, mastering the particular vocabulary that is part of almost any academic discipline, and keeping up with the reading is a huge challenge to even the most accomplished of language students who have not previously lived in a country where the language in question is spoken. Be sure you know what you are getting into and have made a realistic assessment of your ability. If you are struggling to understand, talk to the program advisor immediately and often. You will not be the first student to have encountered this problem and you should be given extra help and/or a change of classes before you are set on a path of irredeemable failure.

Some subjects by their very nature require that you learn in sequence. This is especially true in mathematics, the sciences, foreign languages, and music. In other subjects there may be skills in research, analyzing, and writing that are expected at an advanced level. If you are to be studying subjects that fall in these categories, investigate thoroughly in advance to ensure that you have the prerequisite knowledge and required skills. If you will be continuing study of these subjects when you return home, you will also want to know that what you learn abroad will fit into your plan of study and prepare you for the next level.

Academic structures

From studying the catalog or from the orientation program, your puzzle frame will begin to emerge. You should, of course, know the schedule — when your classes meet and for how long. Calculate the number of hours you will be in class. In the U.S., the usual expectation is that for a three-credit course you are in class three hours a week for the duration of the semester (forty-five hours). Comparing the hours in class will begin to give you an understanding of the role classes play in the educational structure of your host country.

> **Example**: In Scottish universities, students spend less time in class than they do in the U.S. This certainly does not mean that the work is less rigorous, but rather

is an indication of the different role that teachers and students assume. In Scotland, the student must spend a high proportion of his/her time in reading and research outside the classroom.

In some colleges in India, students may be in class for the better part of every day, affording the teacher time to know students well and direct their learning.

Later in your study abroad, you may answer the question about how these different approaches developed and why. Does it have to do with the availability of books, the desire of faculty to have time for their own research, and/or the degree of independence that the culture believes is appropriate for people of college age?

Tools of the trade

In beginning any task, a first step lies in assembling the tools that you will need. In the academic enterprise, there are primary tools you should locate and, if needed, acquire in order to begin your work soon after arrival. In doing so, you will also begin your thinking about how the educational institution reflects and shapes your host culture.

Are you expected to purchase books for your studies, and if so, how many and at what price? Is there a single textbook for a course, or several separate books? What might this say about the availability of books in your host culture and the financial resources of students? Once you have purchased books, take a look at their authorship and place of publication. Are they published in the nation where you are studying or are they imported?

You will want to locate and visit the library. How many volumes does the university own, compared with the size of the library at your home university? To which periodicals does the library subscribe? Where are most of the books or periodicals in the library published? What does this information begin to tell you about the college or university—and culture—you are entering?

Example: In Jamaica, students from Europe or the U.S. are usually surprised that the university libraries and the largest bookstore in the capital city of Kingston are small by comparison with their home institutions. But further examination is revealing. The array of publishers and the countries from which the books come is as extensive as at universities many times larger. As the semester goes on, students learn why this is so. Jamaica has numerous international connections, leading Jamaicans to be interested in the ideas coming from these places. Jamaica is a black nation and obtains books from and about Africa. As a British Commonwealth nation, Jamaica obtains books from Britain and Canada. It is a member of the Organization of American States, and thus is tied to Mexico and Central and South America. Jamaica is geographically near the U.S. and is greatly influenced by it. Similarly, it is only a few miles from Cuba and is therefore interested in the theories of socialism from Cuba and, at least in the past, from Russia. The Jamaican banana industry has a huge economic stake in the policies of the European Common Market. Finally, Jamaica has a large population of people of Indian descent and thus many are interested in India's culture and political life.

In many places and for many of today's students, the Internet is a major source of information. But it is available in varying ways and degrees. What facilities for Internet use are there on your campus? How many computers are there? With what software? Are the electrical power system and telephone reliable? Do students have free access to the computers and Internet? During which hours of the day, and under what conditions? You will want to know this information for your own use, and you should think about the needs of others. As a guest at the university you need to know how many people will use a single computer with Internet capabilities so that you do not offend by claiming more than your fair share of time. Look into the cost, both to you and to the college. You may be accustomed to surfing for hours on end. Such activity may put undue strain on institutional resources and annoy those with whom you must share Internet access.

The understanding of the use of electronic technology on a campus reveals the conditions in the culture, the degree of open access to information, the economic conditions of the nation, and possibly the technological skills of students and faculty.

Preparing for classes

It is a good idea to locate in advance the buildings where your classes will be held. Use your campus tour to observe the facilities. Note which building lies at the heart of the university. What does this tell you about the institution and the culture?

> **Example**: In Japan, many universities have a place set aside to honor the memory of their founder. It may be a garden or room with a bust or painting of the founder, and the area is usually supplied with seats or benches. Students and faculty are encouraged to use the place to contemplate the life and values of the founder. This

speaks to the way in which ancestors are esteemed in the culture.

In many parts of the world, universities founded by a branch of the Christian church will have a chapel at the center of the campus, a location chosen not only for its convenience in the days when daily chapel attendance was required, but also for the symbolism, indicating as it does that the heart of the university is its religious tradition. A striking variation of this is the Luce Chapel at Payap University in Chiang Mai, Thailand. It is a Christian church, indicative of the university's founding and present ties, but its Chinese-American architect designed it in the shape of a lotus flower, a Buddhist symbol for reaching to heaven.

As you become familiar with the campus, take note of its architecture. Identify the oldest and the newest buildings on the campus. Do the buildings reveal a long history, reflecting changing needs, changing times, changing resources, changing tastes and values?

Example: The University of Virginia in the U.S. was founded and designed by Thomas Jefferson, who was himself an architect. As author of the Declaration of Independence and third president of the United States, his fame and importance in American history can hardly be overestimated. The University has perforce built new buildings over the years, but scrupulously preserved the Jefferson-designed section of the campus.

As you observe the architecture, you will also be aware of the equipment. Does the investment of money in buildings and equipment tell you anything about the relative status of various disciplines and fields of study? The answer may be more complicated than appears at first glance.

Example: A beautiful new building dedicated to a particular field of study may be the result of thoughtful strategic planning to serve growing needs in the nation or it may the whim of a particular and very wealthy donor wishing to honor a beloved professor of fifty years ago.

There are universities in parts of the world that by comparison with First World institutions appear to have poor facilities. Yet their graduates go on to advanced study at the world's finest universities and there distinguish themselves and the institution from which they came. If you are studying at such an institution, a central question for you over the next weeks and months will be how this comes about. Is it the selectivity at entrance, the discipline and application of students to their academic work, the quality of teaching? What factors other than resources may contribute to academic achievement? What does this reveal about the culture?

Dressing

Before the first day of class, you should also determine what clothes you should wear. In general, the U.S. is more casual about dressing for university classes than are other countries around the world. In many colleges and universities there is a dress code that may prohibit sandals, T-shirts, shorts, jeans, low-cut necklines and waistlines, short skirts, clothes that are very tight or very baggy, and pierced body jewelry. Even if there is no actual dress code, you can be sure that there are acceptable and unacceptable standards of dress, and that you will be judged accordingly. (If you are in a program that includes volunteer service or an internship, you should be aware that this will apply to your workplace as well.)

You will want to know in advance what the rules and expectations are, rather than be embarrassed because you are turned away or give a bad impression in the beginning. Dress codes come about for a variety of reasons and in a variety of ways.

> **Example:** In Mexico, an orientation director explains to foreign students that the reason for the formality of Mexican dress in many places including universities is that dress has become an important means of indicating that you are rising or have risen in socioeconomic level. To dress in sandals would be to deny the role your university plays in this kind of advancement of its students.
>
> In Africa, body piercing was a part of cultural traditions of the past, traditions now being given up by many people, especially those who have had the advantages of higher education. To see someone from Europe, Asia, or the Americas with these marks is interpreted by some Africans as an insult both to their past and their present.

A word of caution: because a climate is warm and the country may have tourist resorts and beaches, it does not follow that dress is informal at a university or other places of business.

And a word of advice: by dressing in an extreme fashion, you are likely to be judged and isolated from many others, including classmates and teachers. You came abroad to enter into and get to know another culture. Do not put up barriers to achieving that goal by dress that will be considered odd. Dress conservatively, neatly, cleanly, and without show, and you will find yourself being welcomed and included.

Addressing

A second issue for which you should be prepared even before class begins is that of the proper way to address your teachers. In almost no place is it proper to address a faculty member by his/her first name, except in a few colleges in the United States. Your in-country program director may invite you at some point during the program to do so, but do not so presume until you are invited. You should learn the appropriate titles and be sure that you know and can pronounce the teachers' names correctly — a common and expected courtesy in any culture. "Professor" has a very special meaning and status in many nations and should not be used to apply to just anyone who is teaching. Similarly, do not assume that all of your teachers hold doctorates. Various customs prevail in different places.

> **Example**: In Latin America, teachers are addressed by their academic discipline, so that a teacher or administrator might by known as Biológico Rodriguez, indicating his field is that of biology, or Licenciada Guzman, indicating hers is law.

Class behavior and requirements

Once you have arrived — on time! — for your classes, sitting (not slouching) attentively in your seat, prepared with pencil and paper to take notes and otherwise showing your intention to work, you will want to learn just what is expected of you. The teacher will give you information, in print or verbally. If you are given printed material, read it so that you do not ask questions already answered. You should determine early in your term abroad what you are expected to learn and master and when and on what criteria you will be judged. Ask about the form of examinations. Will you be asked to write essays or answer true-false or multiple-choice questions? Will you have any choices on which questions you will answer?

Ask what other assignments you will be given and, again, on what basis you will be graded. Find out not only about length and scope, but about such criteria as writing ability, spelling, punctuation and the citing of references. Do not make any assumptions at this point about the quality of the education you are bringing with you and that being delivered by the country to which you have come. There is little correlation between the economic success of a nation and the educational standards of a particular college or university. One of the questions you may explore further at a later date is just what the nature of this relationship may be. The sad fact is that many teachers in universities abroad, including and perhaps especially those in the developing world, are shocked by what they consider the low level of American higher education.

Example: A professor of literature in Jamaica refuses to grade papers if she notices a spelling or punctuation error, believing that students should have mastered these essentials before entering college. U.S. and British students declare her course to be the hardest they have ever experienced.

In some institutions of higher education, books may be assigned and strongly recommended, but are never referred to by the teacher. This does not mean that they are unimportant or that the teacher has somehow forgotten them. Rather, the assumption is that the student is capable of reading and mastering the contents without help.

Class attendance is disregarded in most European and Japanese universities. In India, teachers keep careful records and include attendance in determining a student's marks.

If you have identified and then acted upon the information you need to begin successfully your education abroad, you have found the puzzle corners and begun to fit some first pieces into place. You have clues about how to proceed and you may even have glimpses of the final picture that your puzzle, once completed, will portray. Remember the conceptual framework for your study: How the educational system both reveals and shapes the culture. You have had a few initial examples. In the next stages, if you are active in your inquiry, the questions and some answers will come thick and fast.

Chapter 3

The Purposes

As your study of higher education progresses through your experience and reflection, the purposes of the system, its structures and methods, will be revealed. When you think about it, you realize that the central purpose of formal education is to prevent your having to discover or develop for yourself what others have already learned. Education is efficient! But in the time allotted to your education, you cannot learn all that could be learned from the vast amount of human experience and thinking that is remembered and recorded. Institutions, individuals, and those in charge of systems make choices about what will be taught. Whether these choices are made deliberately or less consciously, they are made on the basis of the purposes they are meant to serve.

As you reflect on what you see, hear, and read, you will discover what higher education is meant to achieve. As with the system of higher education, you will find a variety of levels, some complementing and reinforcing, others contradicting and counteracting one another, with regard to the purposes.

> **Example:** The stated purpose of higher education in a particular system or institution may be that of developing the skills of critical thinking, but an individual teacher may resist—and judge as poor—the work of students who question the teacher's opinions.

You also need to realize that the rhetoric may or may not match the reality.

Example: A college motto or university mission statement may claim that the purpose of the institution is to serve the society. Yet little or nothing in the curriculum, teaching methods, and structure specifically leads to or rewards service. Faculty members are not promoted through their accomplishments in service. Self-advancement of the student without a concomitant responsibility to the society may be the predominant message of the content and teaching methods of the university.

There are four primary purposes that institutions of higher education claim to serve:

- Transmitting culture
- Conducting research and generating new knowledge
- Inculcating values and beliefs
- Training the future workforce of the nation

Find examples of each of these, and any other purposes you may uncover, in both the rhetoric and practices of your institution. Determine if your institution is unique or at least unusual or if it is representative of the system of higher education as a whole. Draw a conclusion, tentative though it may be, about which of the purposes you have identified are the most important and which play only a small or no role. Finally, look at the overarching question of your study: How do these purposes reflect and shape the culture?

Transmitting culture

Although not often specifically articulated, the primary purpose of higher education is to transmit to the younger generation the major accomplishments and characteristics of the culture, thereby ensuring the continuing appreciation of these accomplishments, the values they imply, and the behavior they are believed to foster. The survival of the culture is at stake.

At the heart of this purpose lies the transmission of the language— its words, its structures, and the thought processes it both generates and reflects— and the cultural patterns that go with it. Teaching students to understand in a sophisticated way the written and spoken word and be able to express themselves precisely and persuasively is a goal that crosses all fields of study. In the study of language, great works are held up as examples of ideas and the expression of those ideas.

Beyond this overarching study of language are many courses in the university that are directed to teaching the student about various aspects of the culture. History, literature, political science, religion, philosophy, business, and the arts are the obvious subjects. In addition to the actual subject matter of the course, there is the transmission of culture that has to do with methods and patterns of thinking.

> **Example**: In teaching the scientific method, students are learning about an important value and practice of the culture having to do with its way of approaching problems and searching for answers.

But in addition to teaching *the* culture (i.e., the culture of the nation), institutions of higher education may have and usually do have courses that teach about other cultures.

Investigating the proportion of courses—and their relative importance in a university catalog—that have to do with the culture of the nation and those that have to do with other cultures may provide important insights into the larger society.

But be aware that there may be different reasons for the choice to emphasize the host culture or other cultures. The inclusion of many courses related to another culture or other cultures may be the result of geographic proximity; of a real or implied threat by another culture and hence a need to be knowledgeable about it; of the presence of immigrants of another culture in the host country; or of confidence that the host culture is strong enough to be flexible and inclusive. Certainly, part of higher education has been the recognition that the cross-fertilization of ideas between cultures is enriching and stimulating. (It is this recognition that inspired your home university to allow you to study abroad.)

The debate between those who defend emphasis on the home culture and those who advocate emphasis on other cultures rages in many if not most universities and nations around the world.

> **Example**: In the Philippines, the debate centers around whether Pilipino or English should be the language of instruction. Of course, both are part of the nation's history, but the one is native, the other a colonial import. Native pride argues for Pilipino; the economic advantage of being the only Asian nation fluent in English argues for English.

As you discover arguments that have occurred on your own or other campuses in your host nation over which parts of the national culture should be transmitted and which other cultures should also be taught, bear in mind that these debates are almost never "pure." That is, philosophical arguments are presented and some people are undoubtedly passionately committed on principle to their position. But the debates sometimes have to do with more practical matters as well, such as the survival of a department or even an institution.

> **Example:** When language teachers argue the need for students to be able to speak a foreign language they are correctly recognizing the global world in which we all now live. They are also ensuring that students enroll in their courses and that their jobs will continue to exist.

Sorting out motives in these debates is almost impossible and, for you and your study, probably unnecessary. What matters in terms of the transmission of culture as a purpose for higher education is the *result* of the debates. It is the argument that wins the day that will have an effect on shaping the future of the culture.

Conducting research and generating new knowledge

Generating new knowledge and new interpretations of existing knowledge has been an important purpose in higher education for at least one hundred and fifty years, so much so that many think of it as the primary purpose. Most universities state that they place a high value on research even if in reality their faculty members do not produce very much.

See what you can deduce about this purpose as you experience the teaching at your host university, and from what you hear and observe. Do your teachers explain what is already known or believed about a particular field, or do they spend considerable time questioning the value of the conclusions reached by others? Do they encourage you and other students to postulate new theories in your papers or is it sufficient for you to accurately report on the writings of those considered by their scholarship to be authorities? Closely tied with this value are the skills required to create new knowledge, new theories, and new approaches. To what degree are the skills of critical thinking— analysis, comparison, connections—emphasized?

Bear in mind that not all fields of study, departments, or individual professors within a field will feel the same about the issue. Be cautious of generalizing from limited experience.

Example: The sociology department of a particular institution may be thought to be on the cutting edge of a field, identifying new issues and seeking ways to see them in a new light. On the other hand, the literature department, uninterested in new writers, may be committed to teaching literary works of the past, literary criticism, and the construction of language in the time-honored ways.

Recognize, too, that research and the generating of new knowledge and new interpretations may be valued at different levels of the university. Ask graduate students at your host university about the expectations for their dissertations and theses. Some institutions may believe, correctly or incorrectly, that undergraduate students do not have a sufficient body of knowledge or skills to launch into new areas of research, but that graduate students, being more fully prepared, should be engaging in such activities.

Example: A distinguished professor at Universidad Autónoma de Guadalajara in Mexico assigns to his undergraduate students readings from renowned anthropologists and examines them on their knowledge of the theoretical constructs of these anthropologists. But he insists that in writing their own term papers his students stick strictly to descriptions. He believes that students must first master the art of accurate observation before they move into interpretation of their own or others' data.

Read about higher education in the nation as a way of judging the applicability of your experience and your institution to the nation as a whole. Look at the justification for public support of higher education that appears in the press. Is research a frequently cited value and purpose?

Finally, look again at our central question: How does this purpose reflect the value of the wider culture and how might it be shaping the culture?

Inculcating values and beliefs

Another purpose higher education is designed to serve is that of inculcating in the next generation a set of values and beliefs. In no topic within higher education is the connection between education and the society more clear. The society recognizes that the college/university years are the formative ones for most students, when their basic beliefs are crystallized, appropriated, and become the way they will define themselves. Students are in the process of making choices about the meaning of their lives, the qualities that will characterize their relationships, the career to which they will devote their time and talent, their understanding of the social order, and their role in and responsibility for it. Here we see in education the ideals that the society holds most dear.

In the case of some institutions, the stated mission regarding the inculcation of beliefs and values is unambiguous, and the organization of the institution and the behavior of the key leaders such as the president and the faculty demonstrate constant reinforcement of these values.

> **Example**: Institutions founded under the auspices of a particular religion; those focused on a particular career that requires a high degree of loyalty, such as military service; or those promoting a particular political, social or educational philosophy may strongly retain and exhibit their principles.

However they were founded, other institutions may today be what the famous American educator Clark Kerr deemed "the multiversity." In these large and often state-sponsored institutions, with their different departments, variety of students, and faculty and president chosen solely for their scholarly or administrative competence, it is more difficult to identify the core values that the institution seeks to instill.

The institution or, indeed, system may pride itself on *not* setting out desirable beliefs and values. But to stop with this interpretation is probably to stop short. Harvey Cox, a famous American theologian in the 1960's, is reputed to have said, "*Not to decide is to decide.*" Refusing to stand in the role of interpreter of values and allowing and encouraging freedom of expression and a wide diversity of opinion is itself a primary value.

To what degree does this value exist in your host university? How does it reflect the values of the wider society? Speculate on the effect of this value in the future. Will universities that have a clear set of values and that discourage other points of view limit the culture's development by their disapproval of new ideas? Or does cohesiveness generate unity of purpose, which in turn fosters development? Do the values implied in the "multiversity" account for a dynamic national life or are they both symbols for and forces of disintegration?

These questions may be asked of any other values in higher education that you identify.

Training the future workforce

A fourth purpose of higher education, one easier to identify and analyze, is that of training the future workforce of the nation. In the Western world, this has always been a function of universities. In the medieval period, when the great universities of Europe were born, the universities were primarily for the education of the church's clergy. Theology and philosophy were not abstract subjects merely to train the mental faculties of students. They were subjects needed to carry on the clerical profession for the institutional church.

Today, as nations and their universities look to the future, they identify the professions that will be needed, and then build educational programs to provide training in these fields. National reports and individual institutional reports are a means of identifying what leaders believe will be the future needs of the nation.

Look at the institution you are attending overseas. What are its biggest and newest departments? Is the university you are attending representative of the majority of universities in the nation?

Remember that students often recognize future opportunities more readily than the older (and sometimes set-in-their-ways) professors and college administrators.

Example: In the 1980's, when Japan's economy was exceptionally strong, students flocked to university business schools, demanding entry. The universities expanded. Now, as the economy has hit troubled times, they are finding enrollment has dropped.

There are economists, including Peter Drucker, a leading authority on management, who have named the private (voluntary) sector of national economies around the world — the one that delivers social services to people in some kind of need — as the fastest growing area of economic opportunity. Needs such as health care for the elderly are increasing and so are those seeking training for the professions that serve them. In a number of countries, new training programs have been created in the last decade for the management of not-for-profit agencies. These degree programs at universities prepare people to direct, supervise, and perhaps even found private agencies for the delivery of social services.

Look to systems as well as to your individual institution to see what jobs and professions your nation is anticipating needing in the future.

Example: Both developing and developed nations are building a form of the polytechnic or community college system. As more and more students enter college and the college/university becomes the means for winning credentials in a field, there is a recognition of the need for mid-level professionals and trained technicians.

Generally offering two-year degrees (the Associate of Arts) or a diploma program, these institutions specialize in training for such areas as paralegal and paramedical services, computer programming, and various technical professions from automotive repair to theater set construction.

You may want to ask how flexible a system is in adapting to new needs. Remember that institutions of higher education are sometimes slow to change.

Example: In India, the rigid structure of higher education has not encouraged the introduction of new subjects. University students had to seek computer training in independent, private institutes that arose outside of the university system to address their desire and need.

A final question on which you might speculate is, To what degree is higher education in your host country preparing students to change careers in the course of their lifetime? Most analysts in both developed and developing countries predict that in the future we will not work at one job or profession for our entire lives but may choose to or be required by the limits of opportunity to change professions. Does the system of higher education recognize this reality and has it adapted its training to accommodate the new work patterns? What do you believe about how the ability successfully to change careers will shape the nation's future? Will those nations and systems that have trained their workforce to adjust and change be more prepared to weather economic and technological change and thus be more successful than those that have not?

Chapter 4

The Systems

From the lower grades to the graduate level, systems of higher education develop in the context of a society, its values and goals. Sometimes aspects of these systems are designed intentionally to achieve certain ends. Sometimes they simply emerge out of the circumstances and needs of a particular time. In either case they both reflect and shape the culture and can therefore be a major clue to understanding the culture, both historically and currently.

In this topic, you will ask and answer four primary questions:

- How is higher education organized and structured?
- What do the organization and structure reveal about who guides and controls various aspects of higher education?
- How does this structure reflect the culture?
- How has it shaped and how is it shaping the culture?

In answering the first two questions, you will, in effect, be drawing an organization chart. But if you are to be accurate, it will probably not be a simple hierarchy. In most systems, guidance, control, and power are exerted at all levels, and autonomy of decision-making may occur at every level from the Minister of Education down to the first-year student.

Example: Analyzing its needs, a nation may determine that more people are needed in a particular profession. Incentives such as scholarships may be created to encourage students to select that profession. However, the students are allowed to choose their field of study and the incentives may not be enough to reverse the previous pattern.

To understand a system, you need also to be aware that the most critical decisions may not be made at the top, but rather in the middle, through the faculty. The tradition of academic freedom, widespread but not universal, ensures that faculty members will not be fired because of opinions expressed in the classroom. In nations with a strong tradition of academic freedom, teachers have enormous power over both the content of the curriculum and the slant within a field of study.

As you set about determining who decides and controls which policies and practices, you will begin answering the third and fourth questions, forming judgments about the relative importance of these decisions in reinforcing the culture as it currently exists or in trying to change the culture.

There are complexities to which you must be alert in using the educational system to understand the society. For one, because educational systems change slowly, they often retain elements and practices long beyond the demise of the circumstances that brought them about. A system may therefore be out of touch with changes that have occurred in a society.

Occasionally, a system changes in advance of at least some elements of the society. Look for disjunction.

Example: The students may have goals and values different from those of the faculty or administration, goals that may be either newer or more traditional.

Another complexity to which you should be alert is that there are really only a few systems of higher education in the world. Some systems are native to the country but most have been imported, either through deliberate adoption or through colonialism. In either case, the system may retain the structure of its original form, or, more commonly, may be mixed with values, goals, and practices of the local culture.

You will be considering these complexities not only in this topic, but also in other sections, so keep them in mind throughout your examination of higher education. You will find that it is these very factors that make your study valuable to your understanding of your education abroad and, through it, your host culture.

Structure and organization

Here you will investigate at least two and possibly three levels: the federal/national level; the level of the individual institution; and possibly the level of the state/province.

Look first at the institution you are attending. How is it organized? What are the major divisions? It will be divided in several different ways, such as undergraduate and graduate schools, departments by discipline, or by specialized methods of teaching. It may be divided rigidly, with faculty and staff working only in one division, or more flexibly in that some or many individuals and units participate in the activities of more than one division.

Example: Oxford and Cambridge Universities and many other British universities, and those derived from a British system, are divided into colleges, so that a student is admitted into the university and then within a particular college. If you are in such a system, you will need to know how the college fits into the larger university. Knowing this helps you also know where to turn for help, and where various policies and procedures are formulated and administered. This arrangement of colleges within a university is a historical development, and one with some interesting variations around the world. The University of Dublin in Ireland has but one college, Trinity College. Even its highest ranking administrators admit to difficulty in sorting out which powers belong to the University and which to the College, since so much of the structure and organization is coterminous.

Now that you understand something about the structure of the institution you are attending, you should turn your attention to the national level. Understand how your institution fits into a national scheme. Does the nation have universities that are publicly financed and controlled and also private institutions that, perhaps, have more autonomy? Is higher education in your host country divided into technical schools and those devoted to research and scholarship? What degrees are offered — an associate of arts or science, a bachelor's degree, master's degrees, the doctorate? Is the institution you are attending a selective institution or one which has open admissions? (There are advantages to attending a less selective institution overseas in that you may experience the host nation in its majority rather than through an elite few who reflect only a small portion of the society.)

Is there a Ministry of Education? Who makes the appointment of the Minister or Secretary of Education and on what basis? Is the appointment the responsibility and privilege of the chief executive of the nation or must the appointment be confirmed by a legislative branch of government? Is there a permanent secretariat or are the staff members political appointees? Is the Minister powerful in determining curriculum, budget, and other such matters, or is he/she relatively powerless?

In large countries and some smaller ones, education may also be governed at the state/provincial/parish level. Where does this system fit in the organization chart you are building? What are the responsibilities of the system at this level?

Guidance and control

One premise of your study is that education has the power to shape a culture. Therefore, a key question is, Who has control of the system? As you build your paper, consider the question of the relation between the degree of control of higher education vis à vis the system of governance of the nation. That is, do countries ruled by a dictatorship also keep tight control of the education system? What about highly centralized governments with a strong democratic tradition? Do stable and well-established governments with a long tradition of participatory government permit a high degree of autonomy to institutions of higher education?

Does the size of a nation affect control at the national level? What other factors may account for the degree of control exercised by the government over higher education?

You will not be able to answer these questions fully within the time and research required for this study, but they are questions worth considering.

Having looked at the national level, you will also want to know something of the working of the institution you are attending and compare it with other colleges and universities in the nation. Who makes which decisions at your university? Is there a governing board (usually called the board of trustees or board of governors)? How are they chosen? What are they expected to do and not do? What in fact do they do? If you can answer these questions you may be miles ahead in your understanding, because the role of the governors — what they should and should not do for the institution — is a frequent and in some cases ever-present problem at institutions of higher education around the world. The usual distinction between policy-making and management has been a source of conflict between more than one board of trustees and chief executive officer!

You will also want to learn something about all the other levels at your university. Who selects, appoints, and evaluates the head/president/principal/vice-chancellor?

Example: In many universities in Japan, the president is elected by a vote of the faculty. He generally comes from within their ranks and is given a predetermined length of time to serve before a new election.

Academic deans, provosts, department chairs, and the faculty members themselves all have responsibilities for policies, procedures, budgets, and other matters.

The system reflecting the culture

Now that you have a picture of the system of higher education, you will begin to think about how it reflects the culture. Do the system's predominant characteristics seem consistent with what you are observing in the broader culture?

> **Example**: In the United States, each institution of higher education has considerable autonomy. There is a department of education in Washington, D.C., with a secretary of education appointed by the president. But compared with other nations, the department and secretary have little control. This pattern reflects what has been a major issue in American political development. Such factors as the size and diversity of the United States and the high value placed on self-determination have been applied to educational structures. It is fair to say that the nation would be highly resistant to national control of the higher education system.

The system shaping the culture

Many famous educators have written extensively about the link between the structure of education and way the society is formed and developed. The American philosopher John Dewey held that one cannot successfully teach participatory democracy in schools that are hierarchical with all power at the top, schools that do not allow students to have a part in decision-making. He held that classroom lessons may be directed to the working of democracy, but that the experience the students have on a daily basis at the school will negate any "book" lessons if there is inconsistency between what is taught and what is practiced.

Example: A current leader in this field is Adel Safty, who heads the Institute for Leadership Studies at the University of Bahcesehir in Istanbul, Turkey. His interest lies in training young people to be leaders for the global society, committed to the care of all people in their communities, and able to lead members of the community to address and solve problems in a co-operative and collaborative way. The education he provides for students to hone their skills involves their working with communities to address various problems. He knows that their future capacity to build a society based on the principles and practices of participatory democracy depends not only on what he and the faculty of the institute might tell these young leaders, but on how they experience his leadership and practice their own.

This is but one example of how a structure and organization determine the future values and practices of a culture. As you proceed, remember that the role of education in shaping a culture comes about as students experience the structure and later apply it to other institutions of the society in which they are involved, whether they do so because it is the only model they know or because they have deliberately chosen it. Of course, some may deliberately reject the known structure, but that, too, is a demonstration of the way education shapes a culture.

Example: In 1997, a major report commissioned by the British parliament was issued, called the *Dearing Report* (after Lord Ronald Dearing who headed the commission). Among the many points, the report called for strong changes in higher education in order to admit a higher percentage of young people into tertiary education and to provide for lifelong learning opportunities. Universities throughout Britain established committees to recommend actions to meet the goals set out in the report and are now and will be in the next few years implementing those plans. One can expect to find noticeable change in British higher education as a result.

But the real test of the success of these measures will not be the changes in the universities, but rather how these changes affect the future of Britain. It was the desired change in British society that motivated the study. As the effects of the *Dearing Report* are measured, researchers will be asking if greater access to higher education means that more in the population have the skills required by our technological age and hence have greater opportunities for employment. They will want to know if more people, realizing they may need to change careers possibly several times in their lifetime, are taking advantage of retraining opportunities and if, as a result, the economy is more resilient in times of change. They will try to measure whether greater access to higher education has had an impact on the national life.

Another example of deliberate efforts to change a system and hence to change the society is to be found in India. In the highly traditional and, some would say, bureaucratic and rigid system of higher education, the University Grants Commission is encouraging the creation of new universities based on new models with new curricula and new teaching methods.

Chapter 5

The History

Two central questions asked by the discipline of history are: How the past has shaped the present and, more speculatively, How the present shapes the future. These are fascinating questions to ponder. But understanding something of the history of higher education in the country in which you are studying is not only an academic enterprise. It is essential if you are to decode its policies, practices, and procedures and make the most of your studies abroad.

When higher education originated

The first question to explore is the roots of the system and of the particular institution where you are studying. When did higher education originate in your host nation? Did it have medieval beginnings, as in the great universities of Europe, or is it of more recent invention? When was the institution you are attending founded? Look for evidence of the history in the ceremonial occasions such as convocations, in the publications, and in the architecture.

Example: Charles University in Prague, Czech Republic, was founded in 1348. A large and beautiful statue of King Charles V, founder of the university, has a central place in the oldest building on campus, the Carolinum. The rites of the university that take place in this grand hall can be traced to the university's earliest days. The ceremonies are formal, recalling its long and distinguished history.

Universidad Autónoma de Guadalajara, as its name implies, is a private university, the first in Mexico. It was founded in 1931, born from the intense and violent ideological and political struggles of the day. Knowing the history of UAG allows the student to differentiate between this particular university and those that are state-founded and supported in Mexico. The student will thereby understand the variety of opinion represented in Mexican institutions of higher education. It also enables the student at UAG to understand present policies and practices by which all students, Mexican or foreign, must abide.

Where it originated

A second and crucial question for you to ask is whether the system you are encountering arose from the influence of an outside culture or whether it is indigenous to the culture, and if so, which culture. Actually, only a very few systems in today's higher education are largely indigenous. Most have been shaped by and today retain in some measure the form of higher education of the empire which colonized the region in which they are located. The period in which higher education largely assumed its present structures coincides with the period of European expansion and colonization. Everywhere these European nations set their commerce and their flag, they also founded institutions of higher education. Quite naturally, they built them on the model of their home nation.

Example: Knowing the history of the period, you can correctly conclude that the nations of the British

Empire—India, the Caribbean, Kenya, and other parts of Africa—and those with a population made up of English immigrants—Australia and New Zealand—have an educational system based on the one developed over the centuries at Oxford and Cambridge. In francophone Africa, on the other hand, universities are modeled after Continental European higher education.

When and how it took its present form

Knowing the origins of higher education in your host country is not, however, sufficient to understand its present realities. You will need to know when higher education in your host country took on its present characteristics and forms. You must identify the influences that have left their stamp on the present structures and practices and that will therefore be a part of your experience. To make the connection to the wider history you need to know whether the influences originated in the colonizing power, within the host nation, or elsewhere.

Example: The United States originally patterned its higher education after the systems of England and Scotland, but western expansion both demanded and permitted new models. One of the primary categories of U.S. colleges and universities is that of the land-grant universities, whose charge was and is to offer education, particularly in the agricultural sciences, to the wider public.

In the English Caribbean, higher education was originally modeled after the British system. In Commonwealth nations, those university and college graduates seeking graduate degrees were most likely to do so in Britain. In more recent years, the proximity to the United States and the large numbers of Caribbean immigrants to the U.S. have made it practical to adapt the system to U.S. practice in order to facilitate easy transfer from one system to another. The University of Technology in Kingston, Jamaica, has managed to develop a scheme melding both traditions, so that the University may accommodate both those planning further study in the United Kingdom and those planning study in the United States.

The medieval universities in Britain and Continental Europe, providing training largely for careers in the church, had evolved by the nineteenth century to focus on what has been described as "the classics." Greek, Latin, and often Hebrew were the mainstay of the curriculum—the tools of learning that gave access to the great secular and religious works written in these languages. There was a defined body of knowledge to which, it was believed, all educated people in the Western world should have access. There were no electives and few choices among areas of emphasis. All students took more or less the same prescribed course of study. Research science went on outside the academy and only as the nineteenth century progressed was it introduced into the life of universities, first through associated institutes and finally into the university and its curriculum. Similarly, recent and contemporary literature written in languages other than classical Latin and Greek first found favor outside the university, then in the extracurricular activities of students such as the debating societies, and only later was incorporated into the curriculum. Teachers generally identified themselves as faculty at a particular institution, and secondarily named the subject they taught. The primary method of teaching was that of recitation, in which the boys—and higher education was almost exclusively for boys—prepared their translations or other exercises. Class time was spent in presenting their preparations for the teacher's comments and evaluations.

Most historians would agree that higher education as we know it today took its shape in the late nineteenth and early twentieth centuries. Disciplines were defined and distinctive method-ologies were developed for each, departments were established, and the professoriate professionalized by discipline. Lecturing replaced the recitation as the modus operandi of teachers.

From the middle of the nineteenth century to the 1930's, Germany was considered to be a fountain of the finest scholarship in the world because of the value placed on the idea of objectivity there. Knowledge was purported to be for knowledge's sake only, not for any utilitarian purpose. This concept of education swept through the universities of Europe and then across the world, challenging and often replacing the older notion of the college/university as a place to build character and leadership for the society and to train for careers. The generation of new knowledge, new methodologies, and new ways of ordering complex reality became a primary function of the university and teachers began to be rewarded not for their success as teachers but for their research.

The present

Look at the various values, structures, practices, and policies of the institution you are attending. Can you identify those of ancient origin, those of the nineteenth century, and those recently introduced? At what point in history did your university and that of the national system take on its current characteristics? To what degree has it been able to change with the times? Is it fundamentally conservative or revolutionary insofar as educational practice is concerned? (In all likelihood it is some of each.) Be specific about the areas in which it has preserved the past and the areas in which it has changed.

Consider the theory put forth by some students of organizational behavior suggesting that innovation tends to begin not at the center of a culture but at its margins. Put differently, the highly successful organization may be satisfied and have no incentive to change. Those truly struggling for survival may be too weak or too frightened to risk change. But those institutions that are essentially healthy but not at the top of the ladder of prestige may seek new ways to build their reputations.

Does the institutional history of your university bear out this theory? What about the history of higher education in your host country compared with other educational systems with which you are familiar?

The future

Finally, you may want to predict how well your institution and the structure of higher education will serve the society and the world in the future. Is it meeting present needs? What have you seen, heard, or read which leads you to believe that its structures and practices will address the nation's needs in the foreseeable future? Are critics calling for change?

Chapter 6

The Curriculum

You will want to look from several angles at what is taught—
the organization, the subject matter, and the points of view
within a single course. No area of higher education reflects and
shapes a culture more than the content of the curriculum. The
subjects taught encapsulate what is cherished by the culture as
the highest knowledge and wisdom of its past and what it hopes
will be preserved, developed, and extended in the future. An
interesting exercise is to examine past catalogs of a college or
university to see how the curriculum has changed over the
years. In many institutions there has been a broadening of
offerings. Institutions do not necessarily respond immediately
to changes in a culture, but you can generally find some
correlation between national history and that of the curriculum
of an institution.

> **Example:** In the mid-nineteenth century in Britain, the
> Sunday school movement arose to teach basic literacy
> skills to working children. There was a great need for
> teachers and the response was the founding of many
> teacher-training institutes. A few remain today, but
> most have become part of comprehensive universities.

As you examine the curriculum of the college or university
you are attending, you are reminded that your institution may
not be representative of the wider culture. You will need to
compare your institution with others in the nation. If you have

already studied the history of your institution you will have clues as to whether the pattern of studies at your university is or is not representative. If you are attending a large and government-sponsored institution, it will more likely represent the interests and values of the wider culture than if it is privately founded and funded.

Example: It would not be surprising to find in a Jesuit-founded and operated university that theology and the history of medieval Europe comprise a significant number of the course offerings. These would not necessarily represent the interests of a large public. To assess the importance of these studies with regard to national values, one would need to analyze the role the Jesuits play in the history of the nation and of the current culture. If the Jesuits are greatly honored, then the topics that are related to their interests and their history would be similarly honored.

Requirements

First, determine if there are any courses that are required of all students for graduation, regardless of the degree and field of study they are pursuing. It is not uncommon for a university to require a course in the history of the nation and in its language. It may be that a foreign language is required or some study of mathematics and science. Increasingly around the world, colleges and universities that have instituted service-learning are requiring a period of service together with the academic preparation for it and reflection upon it. Requirements are most likely the result of hard-fought battles in the faculty and board of trustees, as the deciding powers have argued about what is most important, needed, and valued. You can be sure that whatever decision was reached there were and probably remain dissenting opinions among the parties.

The departments

Look at the organization of departments. What are the largest departments, with the greatest number of course offerings? These are probably an indication of where the institution and its students believe economic opportunity lies. In times of growth, business studies tend to be popular. One explanation for the burgeoning of service-learning is that analysts such as Peter Drucker are predicting that the social-service sector is a fast-growing segment of economies around the world and that there will an increasing number of jobs in this field in future years.

The largest departments also reveal the skills or bodies of knowledge that the culture believes are essential for all educated people to possess. The study of the language comes high on the list. Regardless of students' particular areas of concentration and the careers they plan, they will need to know how to write and speak the language of the culture with sophistication, precision, and grace.

Note how many departments are linked to others through interdisciplinary courses. There has been much criticism over the years of the fragmentation and compartmentalization of knowledge, reinforced by the departmental system. Innovative institutions are experimenting with courses that include the subject matter and methodologies of several disciplines in the hope that students will see connections between various bodies of knowledge.

As an international student yourself, you should also be interested to know how extensive the course offerings are in cultures other than that of the host nation. Are there special departments focused on regions of the world? Which regions?

How do these reflect the current economic and defense interests of the nation? Do you see any relationship between what you hear on the news or read in the newspapers and the courses offered by the university?

Within departments

Next you will want to examine what is taught within each department. Ask yourself what is being emphasized in a particular field and what is omitted or downplayed.

> **Example**: In the late 1950's in the United States, science departments put their attention on physics. The country had been shocked by the Russian success of Sputnik and, in the era of the Cold War, was racing to bring science teaching to a competitive level. By the 1970's and 1980's, the interest in environmental matters meant that science departments were creating and then giving significant attention to the natural sciences.

> In recent years, there has been an increasing awareness of children with physical, mental, and emotional impairments. Departments of education now offer many courses to prepare teachers who will specialize in the conditions, needs and best teaching techniques for various categories of these children with special needs. This is an example of how an educational system is both reflecting and shaping a culture. The courses are a response to the demands of the wider society. But it is equally true that the departments and some of the researchers within them have been leaders in bringing the situation of children with special needs to the public eye and have pressed for changes in the way these children are treated and served.

Within courses

Perhaps most instructive of all are the points of view expressed by professors in their lectures and classes and in the books they select for your reading. Your teachers' opinions may mirror the majority opinion in the nation, but they are just as likely to challenge the prevailing ideas. Can you determine which is true for your teachers?

First, consider the topics that will be treated in the course. In any subject there is a vast array of material that might be covered. The teacher, department chair, head of the institution, or sometimes even the government have made choices about what to include and what to omit. See if you can determine why some topics are emphasized and others neglected or even banned. Do these represent the personal interests of the teacher or are they related to the interests of the wider public?

> **Example**: In the environmental science courses at Ben-Gurion University in Israel, there is a concentration on desert studies. Located in the Negev Desert, the university has a keen interest in the question of preservation and reclamation of desert regions, and their own in particular.

Next, consider the authors of the books you are assigned to read. Discovering where the books were published is especially instructive if you are studying in a nation that imports the majority of its books. Identify the authors. You may find they are scholars at the nation's most famous institutions of higher education. In what journals has their work been published?

Once you begin to read the books, you will discover the particular frame of reference of their authors. What does this show you about the professor's view? Does it coincide or contradict what you have discovered about the views held in the wider society? Most of all, note whether your teacher presents or recommends that you read several conflicting views on a topic. Ponder the ways in which these divergent views reflect or contradict the values held by the society. If divergent views are not presented and are in fact discouraged, what cultural mores or political forces may be at work?

Finally, look to the point of view expressed by your teachers in class. If the topic under consideration is a current and controversial one, you will find articles in the press on the same subjects. To what degree do your teachers' opinions mirror these?

If you are to make the most of your education abroad, you must first realize there are many points of view on a single topic. You should seek out a variety of analyses and recognize the interests of those holding different points of view. If your university setting is not structured to expose you to a variety of opinions, you should find ways of uncovering them. (One reason that service-learning is valuable as an educational experience is that it virtually insures that the student will be exposed to people across the socioeconomic spectrum.) The single most important lesson to be learned abroad is that no culture is monolithic.

Chapter 7

The Teaching Methods

Teaching methods are an important way of understanding a culture because they reflect the ways a culture approaches the acquisition of knowledge and reveal the logical or intuitive systems through which conclusions are reached.

There are five primary methods:

*   The lecture. In this method, the professor prepares a series of talks on the subject at hand, introducing students to the main issues and points of view of various scholars of the subject. The lecture presents an example of the scholarly approach and of the inner logic of a discipline. One hundred years ago it was common to ask students to copy verbatim the words of the professor. This method would be frowned upon today, but it had the virtue of ensuring that the student completed his study with a coherent book on the topic at hand, with little chance for misinterpretation.

    Students generally see the professor who lectures as the authority on the subject and dutifully take notes of the points made in the lecture. Because this method enables a teacher to address a large number of students at the same time, it is popular in large universities and those institutions needing to educate many students on a minimal budget.

- The tutorial. Here the professor acts as facilitator, guiding the small group of students in his/her tutorial to reading material and critiquing the papers students have written for presentation at the "tute." This method, made famous at Oxford and Cambridge, puts the primary burden for learning on the student. Students accustomed to the lecture system sometimes mistakenly believe that the tutor has not prepared for the class because the time spent together is less structured. Sometimes, too, they miss the importance of the comments the tutor has to offer, and, not understanding the teaching method, even appear at the tutorial without the paper they were assigned to present for the tutor's evaluation and comments.

The discussion is a variation of the tutorial. The professor announces the topic for the day, expects the students to come prepared by having read on the subject at hand, and then asks a series of questions to be discussed by the group. At its best, this pedagogy challenges students to think more deeply about the topic, develop a logic as they move from point to point, and be precise and eloquent in presenting their opinions or interpretations. At worst, it is a rambling discussion in which students give ill-informed and ill-formed opinions that remain unchallenged by the teacher.

- The recitation. Class time based on a pedagogy of recitation is spent hearing the students recount their own mastery of a topic, usually from memory. In the past, this method was useful as students were required to memorize long passages of the great works.

The recitation remains in use in foreign-language classes, as students decline nouns, conjugate verbs, and offer their own translations of a reading assignment.

- The laboratory. The method of directing students to conduct their own experiments began in the natural sciences about one hundred and fifty years ago and had become by the beginning of the twentieth century the method of choice by many teachers of the social sciences such as archaeology, anthropology, and sociology. The disciplines developed techniques for field observation and the teacher's role was that of ensuring that students adhered to these techniques and standards. The experiment or observation sometimes begins with a hypothesis that the student then tests, or it may begin with observation from which patterns are later derived and conclusions drawn.

- Experiential learning. Today, all around the world, teachers are utilizing a variety of methods for teaching a subject that rely on the student's having a direct experience involving active practice. Experiential learning is an updated version of the apprenticeship, in which a student in earlier times learned a profession by working under the direction of a skilled practitioner. This method allows the student to apply the subject of study to a "real life" situation, learning from mistakes as well as successes.

One form of experiential learning deserves special mention, for it is gaining many adherents, among both students and faculty around the world. Service-learning unites academic study with volunteer community service in such a way that the service reinforces the learning and the learning informs the service. Many students long to see the world and to get to know people different from themselves, and they thirst to put their education to use for the good of the society. Teachers see service-learning as a way of challenging the students' assumptions, and they believe that the learning is deeper and lasts longer if it's connected to a real situation.

In addition to these primary teaching methods, there are a number of other less practiced but interesting techniques in use. Technology has made possible "distance learning," which allows students and their teachers, and students and their classmates, to be geographically widely separated.

At the opposite extreme, some colleges and universities practice what is called "collaborative" learning, in which the students engage together in a course of study, relying on each other as well as on the supervising teacher. Some institutions have created learning communities in which students of a particular topic spend a significant amount of out-of-class time together, perhaps to learn a foreign language, perhaps for immersion in a topic, but all geared to learning that extends beyond the classroom.

These are the primary means of teaching in colleges and universities around the world today. Rarely is only one method used. Most teachers and institutions utilize a variety of these methods. The combinations and permutations are almost endless.

As you observe and experience the teaching methods employed by your particular teachers, ask your fellow students about their experiences. Are the methods your teachers employ typical? If you are in special classes for foreign students, even if taught by local professors, you may be having an atypical experience of the teaching methods in the country you have chosen for your education abroad.

After you have identified the teaching methods in your host country and the frequency with which they are used, you will want to return to our primary question: How do the methods used in your host country reflect the conditions and culture of the country and how may they shape the future? In making judgments you must be cautious. There are generally several possible explanations for any form of behavior, including the choice of teaching methods. Suspend judgment for a while until you know the culture better. Try to imagine all possible explanations before you arrive at a conclusion.

If lecturing is a dominant teaching method, what does it say about the culture?

Example: Is it a reflection of a hierarchical and authoritarian culture or is it merely a needed method because the large size of the classes makes it the only efficient way to teach? Lectures are often the foundation for a book or journal article. In the late nineteenth century, many books were published with titles such as *An Introduction to Chemistry: Fifteen Lectures delivered at Oxford University.* Could it be that lectures are a reflection of the emphasis put on research at the university? The lecture may be your professor's way of doing two things at once: preparing for class and writing a scholarly book.

In analyzing the tutorial, discussion, or laboratory, there are similarly several possible explanations.

Example: Is the method of encouraging students to offer their own interpretations and conclusions used because the culture values the individual and does not make strong distinctions between the wisdom of the elders and that of the young? Or is it an indication of the value placed on "the scientific method" by the culture?

If you find the recitation in use, it may be so for one or more of several reasons.

Example: In countries where books and paper are in short supply, the teacher may write material to be mastered on a chalkboard and the students asked to commit it to memory through recitation. The culture may be one that traditionally has relied on an oral tradition. It may be that the educational system is frozen in a pattern of a hundred years ago. It could be that the recitation is used because the purpose of education is almost exclusively the transmission of a well-defined set of beliefs and questioning those values is discouraged for political or religious reasons.

You must here be aware of differences between institutions.

Example: The faculty of an elite college or university who know they are preparing those who will assume positions of leadership in the society may encourage behavior that gives evidence of independent thought. The faculty of less prestigious institutions may, on the other hand, be more authoritarian as befitting the place they expect their students to one day assume in the society.

You should also observe distinctions between the ways various students are treated. Almost all teachers will have those to whom they give more attention and those to whom they give less or no attention. If you observe this behavior, ask why it is so. You must, of course, avoid generalizing to the whole faculty or wider society based on your experience with one or two teachers.

> **Example**: The teacher's treatment may, and usually is, based on the responsiveness, eagerness, courtesy, and intelligence of individual students. Sometimes, however, it is based on gender, class, or ethnicity. Individual teachers would rarely state that they treat students differently, but the reality is that at a less than fully conscious level they may allow their inclinations and inherited cultural assumptions to influence the way they treat students.

Finally, you will want to consider how current teaching methods may shape the culture in the future.

> **Example**: Educators around the world are expressing the concern that students are not engaged in the profound issues facing their societies, nations, and the world. They are instituting service-learning in the hope that by exposing students in their formative years to the problems and by allowing them to participate in addressing these problems, they are raising a new generation of leaders who will put their education to use for the benefit of their communities and the wider society.

Chapter 8

The Faculty

You will begin observing the faculty from your first day of classes. See what you can learn about your teachers from your experience with them, through study of the university catalog, and from questions you ask. Of course, you will want to be discreet about questions that may seem too personal and intrusive. If you explain that you are conducting a study of higher education and pose your questions so that they apply to faculty in general and not to the individual, most teachers will be forthcoming in supplying you with information. In fact, you may find that they are pleased to find someone interested in hearing about the joys and disappointments, rewards and frustrations of their work.

A useful question to ask about those whose opinions you are trying to assess is what qualifies them to speak or write on the given subject. You need to know why the person should be listened to and why his/her opinions are worth considering. It might be said that higher education is about just this issue. On any given subject, the opinions of some are more valuable than those of others because of their greater scholarship or experience. You ask this question when you decide to quote or refer to the author of a book in a written paper. You may legitimately ask it of your teachers as long as you do so courteously.

Another way of thinking about the question of how your teachers arrived at their opinions is to consider what the psychologist Erik Erikson identified as the intersection between personal life history and the historical moment. In the same way that the institution of education is shaped by and reflects the culture, so are individual lives. The circumstances of our lives may not decide our destiny or pre-determine our values and actions, but we all are influenced by the time, place, circumstance, and culture in which we are born and in which we live our lives. (One of the reasons you chose to study abroad is that it extends and varies the influences that will shape you, introducing you to alternative ways of seeing the world and expanding your vision of the choices you may make for yourself.)

Qualifications and preparation

A question that everyone interested in higher education wants answered is how, where, and to what extent the faculty were prepared for their work. The degrees held by teachers are probably listed in the college catalog. Is their highest degree a bachelor's degree, a master's degree, or a doctorate?

This may appear to be a simple and accurate way of judging the qualifications of a teacher, but in fact it is not so. You will need to go beyond the mere fact of a degree to ask what the degree means in the general culture and in the various sub-cultures of the university.

In some systems and in many places, the doctor of philosophy (Ph.D.) is not the highest degree commonly held by university teachers. In Britain, the German-invented doctorate has not traditionally been thought to be necessary for university teaching. Many world-renowned scholars at Oxford and

Cambridge have held as their "terminal" (highest) degree the master of arts. This is true for many British-derived systems around the world as well.

Consider, too, those nations in which only a small percentage of the population go from high school to university, and only a tiny percentage of university graduates go on to graduate studies. It may be that faculty in such places do not hold the Ph.D., but they are nonetheless the very brightest and the very best. They were hand-picked, cultivated, and nurtured by their teachers. They may in fact have wider recognition as scholars and greater skills as teachers than those with Ph.D.'s from nations and cultures where these degrees are more commonplace.

Another factor to determine in judging the preparation and qualifications of faculty members is the field in which they are teaching. In some fields, such as the performing arts, the degree may be relatively unimportant. In others, such as history, it may be crucial. In some disciplines there may be further distinctions, such as in a literature department, which might as happily hire a superb writer without an advanced degree as it does those who have made a period of literature the subject of a doctoral dissertation.

A third factor that must be part of your analysis of the degrees that faculty members hold is the institutions from which they hold their degrees. Were all of the degrees or the most advanced degree they hold awarded by the institution in which they now teach? Remembering that even the best of institutions have some mediocre departments and that there are schools with a modest reputation that have some superb departments, you will want to know the reputation of the institution for the field in which the faculty member specialized. And you may need to know if the current reputation was true at the time in which the faculty member studied for the degree.

Finally, you should be curious to know the international experience of your teachers. You, by your choice to study abroad, believe that those who have had the experience of living and studying in another culture have had a richer education than those not so privileged. Ironically, faculty members from developing countries may have had broader international experience than those from the industrialized and affluent nations. The very lack of advanced educational institutions and opportunities at home may have forced them to seek and attain degrees abroad.

> **Example**: One of the authors of this study was invited to speak to an international gathering of faculty held in Canterbury, England. Although fearing that some in the audience might not understand, she chose to make several references to Chaucer's *Canterbury Tales*. To her delight, it was the representatives from India who instantly recognized the allusions and understood the subtleties. They had all gone to graduate school at Oxford or Cambridge!

Personal profile

In addition to knowing the academic qualifications of your teachers, you will be observing personal characteristics such as age and gender, and perhaps you can deduce something about their social class.

Knowing the history of the nation in which they were born and educated and their approximate ages may tell you about the influences on their lives. But remember that a person's response to a "historical moment" may be willingly to accept the status quo, to rebel against it, or to be essentially indifferent to or even unaware of it.

> **Example**: In a profession that in places is dominated by men, female professors are sometimes expected by students to be ardent feminists. While some women adopt this position, others are quite satisfied to go about their scholarly pursuits without any burning interest to change the culture, and if they are role models for the young women on campus they are reluctant ones.

An interesting question to ask is whether there is a mandatory retirement age. If so, what age is it? If not, is there an imbalance between younger and older teachers? How does this shape the culture of the institution itself? Is there an apparently un-bridgeable gap caused by age differenced on the campus? Does the retirement age in any way reflect and shape the larger culture?

> **Example**: In India, the mandatory retirement age is sixty. Yet there is a shortage in the nation of university places for the many students who both desire and are qualified to enter higher education. Many professors would gladly continue their careers as teachers and scholars, but for the regulation. Why was the regulation established? What in the systems and culture of India prevents it from being changed?

Faculty responsibilities and rewards

An ever-present topic of interest and often controversy on a campus is that of faculty responsibilities and rewards. If you were able to drift from table to table in the faculty dining room or, in some cultures, sip tea in the faculty parlor, you would hear discussions — and probably arguments and complaints — about how overworked and undercompensated the faculty is.

The teaching "load" is a key question. In some nations, teaching five or six separate classes each term is the norm. In other places, it may be as few as two. The teaching load is dependent on the economy of the nation and the institution and on the expectations on the teacher for conducting research.

Related to the teaching responsibilities is the question of what is sometimes referred to as "contact hours" with students. In some institutions, the teacher is required to live on or near the campus and to spend a considerable amount of time with students in informal settings. In other institutions, faculty members are on campus and available to students who wish to talk with them only a few hours a week.

As you look at the responsibilities of the teachers, you will also want to know about the rewards they receive. How much are they paid vis à vis other comparably educated professionals in the society? In some countries the pay scale is appalling to the point that one wonders why anyone would choose the profession. In other places, where the system of higher education is nationalized and the national economy is in serious trouble, the professors may not be paid at all for many months. In this case, the university may shut down entirely.

> **Example**: Tribute must be given to those faculty members of Cuttington University in Liberia for their dedication during almost a decade of civil war. Many continued to teach and protect the campus even when there was no salary to be collected.

Important also to understanding the place of the university professor in the society is the process for hiring and promotion. What factors are considered? Does loyalty to a particular point of view, whether academic, religious, or political, figure into the decision about promotion? Are appointments often made on the basis of family ties?

Who makes the decision? Is it made by colleagues in the department, a university committee, the chancellor or president, or is it made by a body external to the institution? Is the young teacher given increasingly high rank for teaching skill, research accomplishments, service to the university, or service to the society?

Faculty status in the wider society

The answers to all of the above questions and others that will occur to you help you understand the place of the college or university teacher in the wider society. Recognize that there may be different points of view in the society. If the circumstances permit you to do so, ask people of the working class what they think of the contribution of university professors to the life of the nation. Some may accord these highly-educated people great honor, even a kind of reverence. Others may sneer at them for being thinkers only and not doers.

You may also speculate on the reasons for these opinions. Does university faculty represent one end of the political and social spectrum and the working class another? In some nations, the universities are thought to be leftist or very liberal in their political positions, while the nation as a whole is more conservative. But the reverse is as often the case. Is either of these true for the system in which you are studying?

As you reach conclusions about the way education reflects the culture, you will realize that cultures are not monolithic, and that the university may reflect only a small part of the culture.

Chapter 9

The Students and Graduates

If you are to end your study abroad with a reasonably complete understanding of your host culture, you must understand your fellow students and, by implication, those who are not privileged to participate in higher education. One limitation of study abroad as it is traditionally practiced is that your most intense and direct experience of the host culture is confined to the university community. You must recognize that you are encountering only a small and elite percentage of the general population and that the majority, and usually the vast majority, of university-age young people do not go on to tertiary education. The picture you form of your fellow classmates is not representative of the culture at large.

Example: In Great Britain today, at most thirty percent of the age cohort proceed to any form of further education. In the United States, the figure is about sixty to seventy percent, but half of these are in community (two-year) colleges where, if they are successful, they will earn an Associate Degree. In many nations, the percentage is well under ten percent. In studying overseas, you are in all likelihood going from the middle or upper class to an institution that is similar if not even more elite.

To form an accurate picture of the wider culture in which you are studying, you must constantly keep in mind those not part of higher education. (One reason for the appeal of international service-learning is that it allows students to meet, know, work with, and better understand not only those who are part of higher education but those who are not, thereby giving the education abroad student a broader experience of and contact with the host country.)

To form your understanding of students and graduates, you should track down the basic statistical information about the university-age cohort. Find out what proportion of the population is between the ages of seventeen and twenty-five. What percent goes to college or university? What percent graduates from college or university?

Preparation

You need to know what preparation students have had before entering higher education. Asking your fellow students is a good way to get acquainted. Most will enjoy recounting their previous educational experiences, regaling you with stories of how they got the better of their teachers and complaining about the system. It is helpful, too, to judge whether they are better prepared for university than you are. Do not assume because you are studying in a developing country that the preparatory schools of your classmates are inferior.

Find out what percentage of children completes primary school, how many go on—or are allowed to go on—to secondary school, and what percentage of those graduates from high school. Indeed, you should know what percentage of the adult population is literate. You may be astounded at what you learn, and find that these figures alone go a long way in explaining the level of development in your host country. You should also

84

look into how these figures have changed in recent years. Is the literacy rate improving or declining? In gathering this data, be aware of the source and the measurements of literacy. Governments, wanting to claim success, have been known to publish records of what appears at first glance to be miraculous improvement. Further inquiry may show that the standards by which literacy is defined are so minimal as to be meaningless.

Does the nation have compulsory schooling? Is it compulsory throughout the country? At what level are students legally permitted to leave school? In some nations, examinations are given at several levels of schooling to determine if a child or teenager may proceed to the next level.

Investigating the age at which students enter university and the age at which most complete the bachelor's degree is a clue to how education reflects cultural and economic conditions.

Example: In Africa, many students enter university at an older age than do those in Europe. Some have spent years saving the money for tuition. Similarly, many take years to graduate, having "stopped out" periodically to earn money or help at home.

In the United States, there are also many older students. Returning to school after several years of working is a common occurrence. Community colleges, which as the designation implies are located in the centers of population, offer evening and weekend classes to make it possible for working adults to further their education. The creation of these opportunities was a recognition that people in today's fast-changing world need to up-grade their skills continually or change their field of

work entirely as opportunities in some fields shrink and
new ones emerge.

Socioeconomic characteristics

To understand your host culture through education, you will
need to know something of the family background of your
classmates and of university students in general. A good way
to begin is to learn about the admissions procedures. Is it by
examination only, or are other factors considered? If it is by
examination, do some students have a distinct advantage over
others because of their previous preparation or because of the
construction of the test?

> **Example**: Many bright black South African students fail
> the entrance examination to the universities because
> their township secondary schooling was inadequate.
> In an effort to right the balance, universities and service
> agencies there have set up tutoring programs to help
> these students pass the examination and thus gain
> entrance to the universities.

If other factors are considered, what are they? Does it help if a
parent was educated at the same university? Do family
connections make it easier to be admitted? What does this say
about how the society functions? It is a society built on
relationships rather than on rules and regulations?

> **Example**: One university head in India confesses that,
> for the two months of the year when the university is
> deciding who to admit, he goes into hiding because he
> is besieged by calls from friends and relatives pleading
> the case of a particular applicant. Obviously, people
> believe their intervention may be of help.

Have you identified any groups that have been officially or informally denied access to higher education in the past? Such groups may be indigenous tribes, immigrants, or women. Are they now discouraged or denied entrance or are they being encouraged to apply? Some nations, recognizing inequities of the past, have programs that assist students from previously disadvantaged groups in gaining university entrance. In the United States, these programs are called "affirmative action." Keep asking the fundamental question of your study of higher education. How do the admissions policies of the university or university system reflect the wider culture? If there is controversy surrounding the issue of admissions, what are the arguments on each side of the issue? How do these reflect the culture? How do you believe these policies will shape the future society?

The graduates

Having looked at the students, you should ask about their prospects after graduation. Do they expect to go immediately into a career in which they will remain throughout their working lives? How many will go on to advanced degrees, and in what fields? Will they pause for work or travel before advancing their chosen career? Will they find work in the community where their families live or must they go far afield? Will they migrate to a city, or to another nation?

> **Example**: Nursing students in Jamaica or the Philippines know that they will earn far greater salaries by emigrating to the United States, Great Britain, Canada, Australia, or another affluent area. Many enter their university training with plans to leave the country as soon as they receive their degree.

A key question in some nations and in some fields is whether graduates can expect to find work commensurate with their level of education. While higher education is certainly the road to advancement, there are examples of nations in which the educational level outstrips the job opportunities.

Example: Many Filipinas with a master's degree find that the only employment possibility open to them in the current economic situation is to become a nanny for the children of the well-to-do in Hong Kong.

Students' expectations are revealing about the dreams and realities of a nation, its culture and conditions.

Foreign students

Finally, as a foreign student yourself, you will want to look at the number of foreign students, the places from which they come, and role they play in university life. Are there frequent references to gobalization in classes? Is the campus generally aware of the international nature of today's world? Is the admittance of foreign students a sign of the university's effort to make its own national students more knowledgeable and aware of the world? Is the university serving a geographic region beyond its national borders, as does the University of the West Indies in Jamaica? Are foreign students given financial aid or are they seen as a source of revenue for the university?

Are the national students eager to make your acquaintance, or are you ignored? Does the faculty seem to welcome you and your ideas and invite you to share information about your country with your classmates? If so, why is this so? If not, why not? Are students from one nation or region more readily welcomed than others? What conclusions can you draw about the wider culture and its desire to be connected to the outside world from the treatment you and other foreign students receive?

Chapter 10

Student Affairs

How does your host college or university involve itself in the nonacademic issues of students' lives? Does it provide services to aid students in dealing with these issues? Does it sponsor activities? Does it regulate and judge their out-of-class activities and behavior?

You will want to investigate the answers to these questions so that you may take advantage of services provided, behave in an acceptable manner, and add a further dimension to your understanding of the culture.

Housing

A primary question, one you will undoubtedly know the answer to long before you arrive, is whether your host institution is residential, providing dormitories and meals, or whether students must find housing in the community. Most European institutions, most in Latin America, over half in the United States, and many in Asia do not provide housing. This may be because the population served is largely local, because the university does not see as its responsibility providing for this primary need, because university-age students are expected by the society to continue living with family, and/or because there is adequate housing to be rented nearby, thereby relieving the university of the expense.

Many colleges and universities, on the other hand, provide housing. They do so for a variety of reasons. The college may be located far from any other available housing and far from the homes of most students. Or it may be that the ideal and goal of the institution is to create a learning community in which students and faculty are immersed in their scholarly pursuits, free of the other distractions of modern life.

Many institutions provide housing choices for today's students, knowing that their students may have different needs. Some students begin their university careers by living in university housing and then move to other quarters a year or two later. Others live at home and later transfer to university housing. Many institutions without dormitories provide a list of available housing options to assist the student in the search for a suitable apartment or boarding house. Some inspect these private houses to ensure that they are safe.

Student services

Exploring the university catalog and asking questions during the orientation program should also help you determine what other services are or are not provided. Is there a Dean or Office of Student Affairs? Does the institution provide personal counseling, remedial tutoring, library orientation, study skills, time management, group dynamics, career counseling or job placement? These services may prove useful to you as you seek to make the most of your education abroad. They are also an indication of the role the university is expected by the society to play in the lives of young adults under their care.

Example: When young people and their parents see higher education as the means to a career, they may expect the college to aid the student in analyzing career opportunities and in finding a job after graduation. But it may be that the society does not see this as the university's responsibility. Query your classmates on how the society provides help to would-be graduates if the college or university plays no role in career development. Is the task left entirely in the hands of parents, relatives, and family friends? Do those whose families are well connected have an advantage over those who have few connections?

Student activities

You will want to learn if there are college-sponsored activities in which you would like to be involved: sports teams, performing arts societies, or organizations focused on special interests such as business or community service. You already know from your home university that these activities provide a wonderful way not only to develop your skills but also to make friends. Are they college-organized and sponsored, or are they organized and managed by the students themselves without direct involvement of the university? If your university abroad has these activities, do take part.

As you discover the activities, continue to ask how the college sponsorship of and student involvement in them reflect and shape the culture.

Example: In Liberia, where love of football (soccer) is the national pastime, Cuttington University and the University of Liberia have soccer teams which command the loyalty of the students. Baseball is played by universities in Latin America as well as in the United States; ice hockey in Canada.

If you have been to Prague, you will know that citizens of the Czech Republic are devoted to classical music, so you will not be surprised to learn that Charles University has a first-rate orchestra. What may be more puzzling to the first-time visitor is that the orchestra of Rikkyo University in Tokyo each year performs Handel's "Messiah" to a full house at the national center for the performing arts. This quintessential Christian work of music is beloved by the non-Christian Japanese, an example of their love for the classical music of the West.

Religious traditions

An important part of most cultures is the religious heritage and current practice of religion. Colleges with religious foundations have a chapel, regular opportunities for worship, a chaplaincy, and related activities. If there is a chapel at the university you are attending abroad, a visit to it at the time of worship will be instructive. You will experience the tradition of which your institution is a part. Because so many customs and values, great or small, emanate from religion, you will find in the religious practice and life of your university many clues to understanding the culture.

> **Example**: Trinity College, in the heart of Dublin, is not Roman Catholic, but Anglican. Seeing the forms of worship and hearing the preaching underscores the differences between the two religious traditions of Ireland and helps those unfamiliar with these traditions and their differences understand something of the religious dissension that has plagued Ireland for many centuries.

In loco parentis

Perhaps the most profound way in which an institution reveals social patterns of the culture is one not always welcomed by students. The institution may act *in loco parentis*, "standing in the place of parents." Such institutions understand their role as that of monitoring and regulating the student's behavior. They have rules that a student must follow in order to remain in good standing in the institution, and faculty or others on campus understand that part of their job is to see that the rules are obeyed.

Almost every institution has a student handbook, outlining the behavior that is expected and prohibited. Some of the rules may seem odd to you at first because you may not understand their purpose or the values that underlie them. You should know the rules and why they have been instituted.

Example: There may be regulations against smoking in certain places on campus. Is this because of the danger of fire, or because the culture generally disapproves of and wants to discourage smoking among young people?

In a prominent institution in Mexico, students are not allowed to wear sandals on campus. (Unfortunately, many U.S. students who attend this institution have failed to read the regulations or take them to heart and find themselves embarrassed by being asked to leave campus to change their shoes.) The international student advisor explains to foreign students that Mexicans use clothing as a sign of their place in the society. University students are expected to convey by their dress that they are no longer uneducated peasants. As a foreign student, you may or may not approve of such regulations and the reasons for them, but as a guest in the institution you are obligated to abide by the rules.

As you examine individual rules, look at the overall level of monitoring of student behavior, and ask yourself what it tells you about the way your host society sees the college years. Are you considered to be a full adult, capable of managing all aspects of your life and therefore needing no supervision by the college or university? Or are you and your fellow students thought to be in a transition stage between the dependence of childhood and the autonomy of adulthood? If so, where along the continuum does the university believe you to be? Is the institution responsible only for offering its students the opportunity for knowledge and education, or does it also take a role in instilling habits of work?

> **Example**: In India, some institutions establish rules to assist students in the discipline of studying. The use of radios may be prohibited during the week because they are seen as a distraction from studying. You may see such rules as merely an annoyance and a limitation on your freedom, but you should also recognize that application to work is considered by employers and graduate schools as one of the great virtues of Indians and accounts, in part, for their success. Teaching the skill of concentration is considered to be one of the strengths of higher education in India.

The answers to these questions, like the answers to other questions posed in this study, are not simple. An institution may see the students as independent adults in many respects but less mature in other ways. The role the university plays in the extracurricular lives of students is revealing of family and related cultural patterns.

As you consider the way your university does or does not provide for students' lives beyond the classroom, and how the services, activities, and regulations reveal the culture, you will want to be aware of gender differences. Are women under tighter regulations and greater supervision than men? Is this a reflection of the practices in the wider society? Are these customs changing? How will the changes shape the culture in the future?

> **Example**: In many cultures, young people live in their parents' home or under the close supervision of their college until they marry and establish their own home. (In some cultures, they may be expected to continue to live in the home of parents or in-laws for a time even after they are married.) Living with family is considered to be a sign of close family ties. When studying in a culture with other traditions, such students are shocked to find young and single adults living on their own, often in a city far from their parents. They frequently interpret this independence to be a "proof" of estrangement in families when, in fact, it may be no such thing. It may be merely that the culture has provided or allowed a less abrupt transition to adulthood than their home culture.

You may want to look more deeply into the issue of the institution acting *in loco parentis*. What does the history of the nation and its cultural patterns reveal about the process of becoming an adult? Some would say that separation from families in early adulthood has been an accepted and even expected part of cultures made up largely of the descendents of immigrants who left their families to begin a new life in a new place and in nations where people have had to seek employment and opportunity far from home.

Chapter 11

Evaluation

Higher education is about evaluation — of you, the institution you attend, the particular system you experience, and higher education in general. It is society's current means of determining if you and other students know enough to do a particular job or assume a certain place in the society. But it is not a simple matter of pass or fail. There are gradations at each level of evaluation and not all in a society or system agree on the evaluations.

Example: In the United States, a popular periodical called *US News and World Report* each year rates U.S. colleges and universities. Presidents are fond of criticizing the report as superficial until their institution is highly rated, at which time the magazine report is touted as the pinnacle of sound evaluation.

Evaluation of you—the admissions process

Evaluation of the student begins before entering the college or university. The secondary school diploma, courses studied and grades achieved, and the score on an entrance examination including proficiency in the language of instruction are the primary means by which a student is admitted to a particular university. Other special qualities such as leadership, athletic ability, talent in the performing arts, or other personal characteristics may also be considered.

But it would be naïve and inaccurate to assume that these are the only criteria. Family connections and the ability to pay the tuition remain significant in many nations and institutions. In some places, gender is a factor in university admissions.

See what you can learn about the admission system in your host nation and at your host institution. Continue asking the question How does this system reflect the culture?

> **Example**: What do you observe about who enters college or university? Does your research indicate that social class, economic difference, ethnic identity, or gender play a role in who is admitted? Is this consistent with the values you are observing in the society? Are admissions based on test scores alone, and is there any indication that the tests put some groups of students at an advantage or disadvantage?

Evaluation of your work

Knowing how you are to be judged and graded is essential to academic success. Most teachers spell out the criteria early in a term, but if your professor does not do so, you must ask. If the criteria are reasonably uniform across the institution, the teacher may assume that all students understand them, forgetting that as a foreign student you are new to the system.

You may assume that the quality of the papers you write is a major determinant of your final grade. You will want to understand clearly what is expected in writing papers. You should especially determine the customs and forms for citing the work of others. These customs vary from country to country. You do not want to find yourself accused of plagiarism.

Example: In some systems of higher education in Asia, collaborative work among students is normal. The written reports they produce may be very similar as a result of their collaboration. A teacher who expects students to work independently of one another may believe that a student with work similar to that of a classmate has cheated.

A second major determinant of your final grade is your score on examinations. You should ask about the form the examinations will take and have some idea of the material to be covered.

Example: U.S. students assume, usually correctly, that the material covered in class lectures and discussions is the most important and therefore will be featured prominently in an examination. In universities abroad this is not always the case. Especially in the tutorial system, students may be advised to read a particular book or investigate a particular question. The class time may be devoted to other topics, but out-of-class reading may be a subject of the testing.

You should also know who designs the examination. It is not always the teacher. There may be an examining board external to your particular class or external to the university itself. This is particularly true if you are studying overseas not just for a term or a semester, but for a degree.

In determining a grade, teachers sometimes use other factors such as class attendance, class participation, and oral presentations. If you are in a program that requires any form of experiential learning, you must be clear about how your achievements and the satisfaction of your supervisor with your performance fit into your final grade.

While it is always best to plan to complete work by the deadline, you may also want to ask if late work is accepted and under what conditions. Some teachers deduct points from your final grade for papers that are handed in after the due date.

Evaluation of the institution

Colleges and universities are classified in a number of different ways: as public (state supported) and private; by specialties such as agriculture or business; and by the overall quality. The first question to be asked of any institution is, Is it accredited? In almost all countries the accrediting body is the national ministry of education. The United States is unique in its system of accrediting by regional associations independent of the government. In many nations, the national legislative body grants the institution a charter to operate and the ministry of education periodically reviews the institution. Accreditation means that an institution has been inspected and found to meet the criteria expected of an institution of higher education. It is a way of assuring the student and future employers that the institution has advertised itself truthfully and that it can, will, and does deliver a satisfactory education. Losing accreditation is often tantamount to closing the institution since few students would elect to attend and invest in a college or university not recognized as meeting minimum standards.

In many countries there are other organizations which also give some sort of formal recognition. These may be professional societies or associations of similar institutions.

In addition to these formal means of evaluation, there are more informal but powerful means by which an institution is judged. Those who are familiar with higher education in their nation will happily rank the primary institutions of the region. They base their rankings on such factors as the age of the institution, its facilities, the fame or at least success of its graduates and professors, and the research generated by the university. But you must recognize that these informal judgments may or may not accurately reflect the quality of the education.

Example: In the United States, when the general public and even professional educators are asked to rank universities by departments, Harvard University consistently wins the top rating even in areas for which Harvard has no department.

Furthermore, the public is often seriously out of date in evaluating an institution. Alumni may base their ranking on memories of their own university years rather than on the current reality. An institution may bask in past glories for many years.

As you come to know your institution and the reputation it has, ask yourself how both the formal system of evaluation and the informal one reflect the culture.

Example: In some nations, a charter may be revoked or approval denied if the institution is not meeting the political guidelines for supporting the regime in power.

An institution specializing in advanced technology or research science may be judged by the public to be superior to one specializing in agriculture if these are more highly valued by the society.

Evaluation of the system

You will also want to look at how the educational system is viewed in comparison with those of other nations. Almost everyone today believes that education is the key to success, and so it is no surprise that a nation's status in the world community is a reflection of the way the world views its educational system.

But you will also read and hear criticism of an educational system as too strict, too permissive, incoherent, conservative, or liberal. There is no perfect system just as there is no ideal institution. Think about the praise or criticism as a reflection on the values of the speaker or writer, just as you think about the system's characteristics as a reflection of the culture. How widespread are the criticisms? Which groups of people offer which criticisms?

Evaluation of higher education

A final question as you think about evaluation of higher education is how the university and the knowledge it transmits and generates are viewed by the wider public. In some cultures, the university and its professors are almost universally admired. In others, including the United States, there is a strain of anti-intellectualism in the culture in which common sense and practical action are more highly regarded than abstract "book learning." Do you detect any such judgment of higher education in the country in which you are studying. If so, do you know its origins? In what groups of people is it the strongest?

There are other reasons a people may judge higher education harshly. They may feel they are taxed for an institution that serves primarily the rich. They may disagree with the political views predominating at a given time in the universities of their nation. They may disapprove of the behavior of students or the values the faculty espouses. On the other hand, admiration may reflect the belief that it is the university educated who have the most power, are the most civil, or best serve the nation.

If you meet people with strong and various opinions about higher education, you might want to write a few case studies about how they arrived at their good and bad opinions of higher education.

Afterword

You are nearing the end of your study abroad. We hope you have had a wonderful, eye-opening, life-changing time. Soon you will go home, with many exciting tales to tell. Your parents, professors, and friends may not comment openly on the change in you, but they are likely to notice that you are now more confident, more knowledgeable, and more sophisticated.

Your greater sophistication will come in different forms — the use of a foreign language, your understanding of a different government, your ability to make your way around big cities and various means of transportation, your taste for new foods.

One of the most important and sophisticated skills that any person can possess, and one which we hope this assignment has helped you to develop, is the ability to analyze and understand a culture, your own and others.

Being able to enter into the mind-set of another person or group of people, especially those different from yourself, is the mark of the truly educated person. We read literature, study history, learn a foreign language, tackle mathematics, wrestle with philosophy, listen to music, look at art, travel to new places, and meet new people in order to extend our own personal experience, thus sharing, insofar as we are able, in the experience of others. The more we do these things, the richer our lives become.

Further, we take these experiences, whether direct or vicarious, and put them into an order as a way of making sense of complex

107

and contradictory experiences. The various academic disciplines create theoretical constructs to help us think about and understand what we see, hear, and read.

What you have done in this study is examine how one of society's most important institutions—education—reveals the dominant characteristics of the culture. Recall the jigsaw pieces with which you began. Now you have ordered and arranged the pieces of your education abroad so that a complete picture has emerged. All of us as human beings are the product of the intersection of our individual life history and the historical moment. Where and at what time in history we are educated influences greatly who each of us is and becomes. (Notice we did not say "determines"—you are free to make choices.) You, for example, chose to study abroad rather than remain at home, then you chose to study in one country rather than another, at one institution rather than another, in one program rather than another. If the study abroad experience is as important to you as previous students tell us it has been for them, then your education and perhaps particularly your education abroad will shape you and the role you play in your society in the future.

But your study has given you an even greater understanding and skill than realizing how education in all its aspects shapes and reflects a culture. We hope and believe that you have developed the highly sophisticated skill of recognizing where and how another person or group of people has formed opinions and developed cultural beliefs and patterns.

When you return home, your family, friends, and college are likely to see you not only as more sophisticated, but as a leader in a way they have not before. Why would study abroad—and this study of higher education—develop your skills as a leader?

It is the naïve and unsophisticated person who believes that we are all alike and that other people are likely to see an issue just as he or she does. People who are educated and sophisticated in their thinking are those who realize that another person, group, or nation may see things very differently. When you can identify the difference (not always easy) and see how the person, group, or nation came to think, believe, and feel as it does, then you have taken the first step in learning to live cooperatively, happily, and peaceably together, and when there is conflict, work out a negotiated settlement so that everyone benefits. This is the very essence of leadership.

And this is a skill which can be applied to specific daily situations as well as to large international issues. When you are joined into another family — through a short visit or a lifetime marriage — you can apply your skill of analyzing a culture with different practices, values, beliefs, and customs from yours. Every business has its own culture and companies within a single business have a special version of it. Recognizing a culture's characteristics, how its past shapes its present and its present will shape its future, helps you decide the extent to which you will conform or challenge it.

Learning all this is why study abroad is valuable. We hope this study has enriched your experience abroad and that you find it a useful lesson in the multitude of new cultures you will encounter throughout your life. We hope, too, that you will use this skill and the leadership it implies for the good not only of yourself but of your community, your nation, and the world.

Linda A. Chisholm   Howard A. Berry

About the Authors

LINDA A. CHISHOLM is a founder, with Howard Berry, of The International Partnership for Service-Learning and is now its president. She attended Vassar College, holds a B.A. in History and an M.A. in Renaissance and Reformation History from the University of Tulsa, and a Ph.D. in History and Higher Education Research from Columbia University. She has been awarded the D.D. (Hon) from General Theological Seminary; Doctor of Human Letters from Cuttington University College in Liberia; and a University Fellowship from the University of Surrey Roehampton, England. Dr. Chisholm served as the president of the Association of Episcopal Colleges from 1987 to 2000 and was the founder and first General Secretary of Colleges and Universities of the Anglican Communion. She is a trustee and former chair of the United Board for Christian Higher Education in Asia; serves as a trustee of the Harvard-Yenching Institute; and is a member of the International Association of University Presidents. She is the author of *Charting a Hero's Journey*. Dr. Chisholm is a member of NAFSA: Association of International Educators.

HOWARD A. BERRY (1932–2002) was cofounder and first president of The International Partnership for Service-Learning. He received his A.B. in history and philosophy from Fairleigh Dickinson University; completed a Special Tutored Project in international and comparative education at Oxford University; and pursued doctoral studies in history and political science at New York University. He was awarded the honorary degree of Doctor of Humane Letters by Cuttington University in

Liberia; the Master of the University honorary degree by the University of Surrey Roehampton in England; and the Distinguished Service Award from the University of Technology in Jamaica. He was named Professor Emeritus by SUNY Rockland Community College, where he had served as professor of History, Director of Intercultural Studies, Languages and English as a Second Language, and president of the Faculty Senate. Professor Berry was an invited member of the International Association of University Presidents; a member of NAFSA: Association of International Educators; and a member of the Board of Directors, IVPA: International Volunteer Programs Association.

Response Form

Please help The International Partnership for Service-Learning and NAFSA: Association of International Educators evaluate the usefulness of this book by copying, completing, and returning the form on the following pages.

If you are a student and wrote a paper based on the book, we would like to see it. If you send us a copy and your contact information, we we will refund to you the price of the book and shipping.

Response Form

UNDERSTANDING THE EDUCATION—AND THROUGH IT
THE CULTURE— IN EDUCATION ABROAD

❑ I am a study abroad advisor
❑ I am a foreign-student advisor
❑ I am a U.S. student who studied abroad
❑ I am a foreign student in the U.S. from _____
❑ Other

I am attending or work at a college or university in the U.S. that is:

❑ Public	❑ Under 5,000 students
❑ Private	❑ Over 5,000 students
❑ 4 year	❑ highly selective
❑ 2 year	❑ somewhat selective
	❑ open admissions

If you are a student, where did you study abroad?

_____

If you are an advisor or faculty member, what is your area of expertise?

_____

How did you use this book?
❑ As the syllabus for a credit-bearing course
❑ As a requirement but without credit
❑ As a guide to writing a paper or journal about my education abroad or in the U.S.
❑ As a guide for students who study in a foreign country under my guidance
❑ For my own edification

How useful did you find this book?
❑ Very useful
❑ Somewhat useful
❑ Not useful at all

Did it help you (or your students) avoid academic difficulties?
❑ Yes
❑ No

Did it help you (or your students) understand the culture through the study of education?
❑ Yes
❑ No

Are you (or your students) finding a use for the skill of analyzing culture through its institutions?
❑ Yes
❑ No

Optional:

Name _____

U.S. Institution _____

Address _____

_____

E-mail _____

Phone _____

Please return by mail or fax to:
The International Partnership for Service-Learning
815 Second Avenue, Suite 315
New York, NY 10017 USA
(212) 986-0989 tel   (212) 986-5039 fax
info@ipsl.org   www.ipsl.org